One-Weekend Country Furniture Projects

One-Weekend Country Furniture Projects

Percy W. Blandford

TAB BOOKS

Blue Ridge Summit, PA

FIRST EDITION
FIRST PRINTING

© 1991 by **TAB Books**.
TAB Books is a division of McGraw-Hill, Inc.

Library of Congress Cataloging-in-Publication Data

Blandford, Percy W.
    One-weekend country furniture projects / by Percy W. Blandford.
        p.   cm.
    Includes index.
    ISBN 0-8306-6702-4   ISBN 0-8306-8702-5 (pbk.)
    1. Furniture making.   2. Country furniture.   I. Title.
TT194.B54   1991
684.1—dc20   91-6609
                                                             CIP

TAB Books offers software for sale. For information and a catalog, please contact
TAB Software Department, Blue Ridge Summit, PA 17294-0850.

Acquisitions Editor: Kimberly Tabor
Book Editor: Marie G. Bongiovanni
Production: Katherine G. Brown
Book Design: Jaclyn J. Boone   HT3

Contents

Introduction

The making of furniture is among the most popular of an enthusiastic wood-worker's shop activities and is likely to be the most appreciated by the rest of his or her family. Making a piece of furniture for the home and being able to look at your creation gives a tremendous sense of satisfaction.

Some furniture making requires a considerable amount of skill and may be very time-consuming. It is not always easy to judge whether you will be able to find the skill and time for some projects. This book is an attempt to bring together 49 furniture projects that might be completed in one weekend.

Obviously, with varying degrees of skill, vastly different kits of tools and unknown time available in a weekend, not every person can expect to achieve the same results. However, it is assumed that a weekend means a working time of 12 hours or so. It is also assumed that prepared wood in the sizes mentioned in the materials lists will be available beforehand.

If you have an elaborately equipped shop and the skill to make use of it, you can expect to do much more in a given time than a beginner with a few hand tools and a makeshift bench.

There should be something for everyone among the projects in this book. Some of the simpler items might take a sparsely equipped beginner the whole weekend, but give him a very satisfied feeling at the end of it. Some of the more advanced projects might take the well-equipped expert all the time he can find, then he will achieve an equally satisfied feeling commensurate with his skill.

Although some traditional joints are used, many projects involve simplified construction, so do not be put off by a project that appeals to you because it seems too advanced. Look at the suggested construction. You may find the project has been arranged to bring it within your skill range. In any case, we all do well to extend our abilities to the utmost. Do not be intimidated by size. Complication and difficulty is not related to size. Some big projects are the easiest in this book.

The book has been divided into chapters for convenience in grouping, but there are some projects that are appropriate to more than one chapter. Check the book as a whole when looking for a particular type of furniture.

Unless otherwise marked, sizes on drawings and in materials lists are in inches. Widths and lengths of solid wood are quoted as finished sizes, but a little extra may be allowed on lengths for trimmings. Materials lists are located near the end of each project

Read chapter 1. It is your guide to making the best use of your weekend. Then start on as many projects as appeal to your interests or needs. Whatever your facilities in skill or equipment, you will enjoy the work and its results.

1

Preparations

While this book is a collection of detailed designs intended to show you how to make pieces of furniture in one weekend, whether you can or not depends largely on your planning and preparation—those are the key words. If you wish to tackle a project in a more leisurely way, it may not matter if something delays progress or you have to go to the lumber yard or hardware store for a missing item. If you are aiming to produce a good piece of work in a reasonable time, without problems along the way, you must think the job through. All the material must be ready and you must know the order in which to perform various operations.

Make sure every piece of wood is there. It does not matter if you have too much. It would hold up progress if you had to interrupt work to get a missing piece. The materials lists give finished widths and thicknesses, but usually a few extra inches of length for exact cutting. You may be able to use wood of slightly different sizes, but make sure you know how to allow for this in the general design.

You may need dowels. Make sure they match your available drills. Similarly, make sure there are more than enough nails and screws of the right sizes, and the drills to match. Do you have enough of the right sort of glue? What about abrasives and finishing materials? Then there is hardware, such as hinges, knobs and catches. You may need to prepare wood to match them, even if they are not attached until later.

If the project you select needs wide boards and you have to glue pieces to make a width, you may choose to prepare these pieces in advance, so the glue will have time to harden. The alternative is to do all this gluing on the first day and allow hardening overnight.

There are sections of wood and sizes of screws and nails common to many projects. If you want to make several items of furniture, it may be convenient and more economical to buy some things in quantity. It costs less, proportionately, to buy a complete sheet of plywood than to have several pieces cut. Buying enough long pieces of wood to cut yourself will be cheaper than buying a few short pieces several times. Nails and screws of many sizes are good stock and worth buying in bulk.

Think about the tools you need at every stage. You can do a surprising amount of work with very few tools, but you must have the basics. For instance, you must have tools to saw and plane, but it does not matter if they are for hand or power use. Marking out accurately is important, but you may improvise. The corner of a plywood sheet serves as a square. A strip of wood makes a straight-edge. What is important is that you know what tools will be needed as you progress.

Study the step-by-step instructions in relation to the drawings. Think through the construction. It is always easier and more expedient to do things to separate pieces of wood, when possible, than to wait until they are assembled before drilling, cutting or performing some other operation. It may be advisable to sand and take off sharp edges before a piece is built in. This is particularly so with some inside surfaces. Try to constantly anticipate the step after the next, and do all you can to prepare the way.

If it is important that several pieces match, mark them all together—usually side-by-side, with a square across. Some may then need additional marks, but get vital matching distances drawn. If several similar joints have to be cut, do this together, usually working the same stage on all joints before moving to the next operation.

To complete a project in a two-day weekend, you may have to take advantage of the overnight break, particularly to let glued joints harden before further work, so you should make and assemble these parts on the first day. In many assemblies, such as a four-legged framework, accuracy may be easier to obtain if the glue on opposite sub-assemblies is allowed to harden before pieces are added the other way.

Symmetry and squareness are important—errors of shape are very obvious to any observer. Do not try to square a large framework with a small try square. It is more accurate to compare diagonals between opposite corners or other matching points. You could use a tape rule, but marks on the edge of a piece of wood opposite points that should be at the same distance are less prone to errors. This works on a tapered symmetrical assembly as well as a square one. Remember to check squareness as viewed from above, at the bottom as well as the top.

How much can be done in a weekend depends on you, your ability and available equipment, but it also depends to a large extent on your forward planning. Adequate preparation will ensure efficient working and increase satisfaction at the end of your weekend woodworking.

2

Tables

There is always a need for tables. With our modern style of living we need surfaces to put things on. A table may be at a height for use when sitting on a chair or standing to eat, write, do hobby work or play board games. A smaller table at about the same height may be used for display or to serve from, or it may sometimes be joined to the bigger table to accommodate more people. Lower tables, often called 'coffee' tables, may be used at a chair side or for sharing drinks or magazines. Variations are used in bedrooms and elsewhere. Others, usually more robust, are used outdoors. Some types may be made to fold or take apart for convenience in storage.

The scope of table making is vast. Some of the larger and more advanced table designs involve too much work for a weekend, but a large variety of tables could be made within about 12 hours. If boards have to be glued to make up widths, that may have to be done in advance, but most tables, even large ones, are straightforward and not difficult to build.

The structures of many tables can be divided into units or sub-assemblies. If you work systematically prefabricating these parts and then put them together, you should finish a table to be proud of.

SHELVED COFFEE TABLE

A small table used for snacks, as a chair side rack or as a repository for odds and ends, soon becomes crowded, and it is difficult to find space to put down a mug of coffee. A shelf underneath will provide extra space for many items and keep the top clear enough for anything in current use.

This table (FIG. 2-1) has a shelf underneath separated from the top by a central spine, which provides rigidity. The outlines are curved, to give an attractive and less austere appearance than if they were kept straight. The sizes (FIG. 2-2A) should suit most needs, but if you wish, you could alter them by a few inches.

Construction is intended to be with solid wood, which will probably have to be glued-up to make the widths. It would be possible to use particleboard. The moderate curves will take iron-on veneer edging. Plywood could be treated the same way, but solid hardwood will provide the most attractive appearance. For a playroom or den you might consider softwood with a painted finish.

Prepare sufficient wood by joining pieces to make up widths. Clean off the joints and plane or sand the surfaces, if necessary.

Mark out the top, while the sides are straight, with the positions of the legs on the underside (FIG. 2-2B).

Fig. 2-1. This coffee table has solid parts doweled together and a convenient shelf, which provides stiffness.

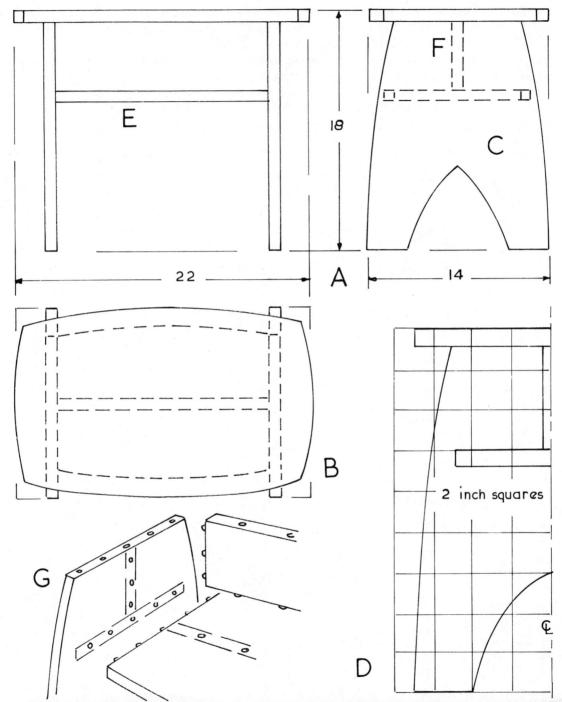

E

18

22

A

F

C

14

B

G

D

2 inch squares

⌀

Fig. 2-2. Main sizes of the shelved coffee table and the arrangement of dowels.

Draw centerlines both ways. Cut a card template of one quarter of the top outline (FIG. 2-3A) and use this against the centerlines to mark the shape.

Cut the shape and smooth the edges. You could mold them, but you will probably consider the shaping is sufficient decoration. A slight rounding of the edges and corners should be all the treatment needed.

Make the two legs (FIG. 2-2C). At the bottom they reach the full width of the

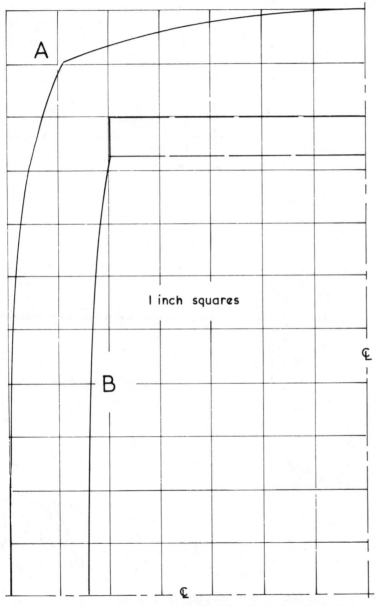

Fig. 2-3. Shapes of the top and shelf of the shelved coffee table.

Materials List for Shelved Coffee Table

(all finished $3/4$ inch or $7/8$ inch thick)

1 top	14×24
2 legs	14×19
1 shelf	12×20
1 spine	$5\frac{1}{4} \times 20$

top, but their tops are 2 inches in (FIG. 2-2D). Cut the shapes and mark on the positions of the shelf and spine.

Make the shelf (FIG. 2-2E), which has a curve parallel with the top (FIG. 2-3B). Treat its edge in the same way as the top.

The spine is a parallel strip (FIG. 2-2F).

Prepare all the parts for dowels (FIG. 2-2G). Use $3/8$-inch dowels and space them at about 3 inch intervals at the ends and about 4-inch intervals along the spine.

Sand all parts before assembly. See that all holes are clear and deep enough.

Join the shelf to the spine first, with glue and dowels. Join these parts to the legs. Check lack of twist by sighting across the tops. Join this assembly to the inverted top, then either clamp or put under weights while the glue sets.

Finish with stain and polish if hardwood, or paint if softwood.

ALL-SHEET COFFEE TABLE

Most small tables are made with strip or square wood framing under the top. This coffee table (FIG. 2-4) differs in being made completely of sheet material. It

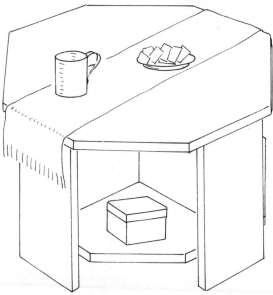

Fig. 2-4. This octagonal coffee table is very rigid and is made entirely from sheet material.

could be plywood or veneered particleboard, finished with iron-on matching edging. There are divisions below and above a shelf, which is supported between four legs—all in the same material. With careful cutting it is possible to cut all parts from little more than half a standard sheet of plywood.

Most joints are made with dowels. You could use ⁵⁄₁₆-inch or ³⁄₈-inch diameter dowels at about 3-inch spacings. Alternatively, you could use screws, counterbored and the holes filled with plastic plugs, which will make decorative patterns. For the joints between the shelf and the division, the screw heads will not show and they can be driven without counterboring.

As drawn (FIG. 2-5) the octagonal top is 24 inches across and about 16 inches above the floor. The same method of construction could be used for tables of

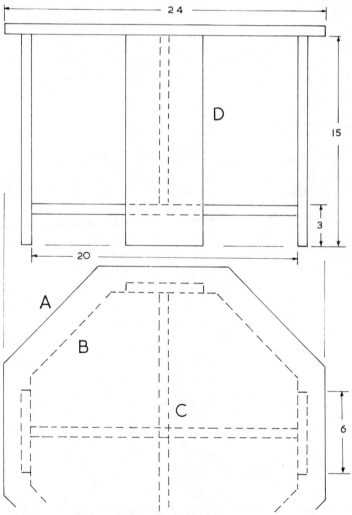

Fig. 2-5. Main sizes of the all-sheet octagonal coffee table.

widely different sizes. Besides the octagonal top there is a shelf of similar shape, but 20 inches across. These two parts determine the sizes of the other parts and should be made first.

Mark out the top (FIG. 2-5A) by any of the methods of drawing a regular octagon. In this case, a simple way is to draw a square of the overall size, either on the material or on a piece of paper to use as a template. Draw lines between opposite corners and measure half of one of these diagonals. Measure this distance from each corner along each edge, then join the marks. Check that you now have eight equal-length sides before cutting. Cover the edges with iron-on strip.

Mark and cut the shelf octagon (FIG. 2-5B) in the same way.

Cut the two divisions (FIG. 2-5C and 2-6A and B) to size, with the distance across the same as the parts of the shelf they have to match.

Cut half out of the center of each piece so they can be fitted together. This joint does not have to provide strength in the finished table, but the parts should fit closely for the sake of neatness.

Drill for screws through the shelf and join it to the crossed divisions.

Make the four legs (FIG. 2-5D and 2-6C). Use iron-on edging on the long edges.

Mark and drill for dowels into the shelf and the divisions.

Join the legs on. See that all top edges are level and the bottoms of the legs will stand level on the floor.

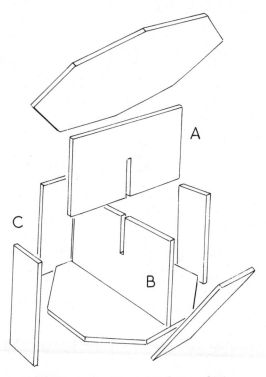

Fig. 2-6. How the parts of the all-sheet coffee table fit together.

Locate the assembly on the inverted top and mark the positions of dowels. It should be sufficient to put two dowels in the top of each leg and dowels at 3 inch intervals across the tops of the divisions.

Check that all edges are smooth and there is no sanding to be done, then glue on the top, using weights or clamps to get tight joints.

If you have used plastic veneered particleboard there will be no finishing required, but if it is wood veneer or plywood, apply an appropriate finish.

Materials List for All-sheet Coffee Table

(plywood or veneered particleboard $\frac{5}{8}$ inch or $\frac{3}{4}$ inch thick)

1 top	24 × 24
1 shelf	20 × 20
2 divisions	12 × 20
4 legs	6 × 15

NESTING TABLES

A group of three tables that fit into each other needs minimum space, but the two inner tables can be taken out when you need their extra area for coffee or refreshments. The usual set of nesting tables are of compact coffee table size. This set offers a wider range of sizes (FIG. 2-7). The large table has a top 20 inches by 30

Fig. 2-7. Three small nesting tables, which fit so they can be lifted together.

inches and stands 20 inches from the floor, so it could be used as a side table or among a group of chairs for refreshments, magazines, or books. The second table is nearer the usual coffee table size, measure 16 inches by 22 inches and 18 inches from the floor. The small table might be used as an individual coffee table, but it could also be a seat or stool, with its top 12 inches by 14 inches and a height of 16 inches.

The two inner tables hang when they are nested, so you can take them with you if you lift the large table. Of course, the nest of tables does not have to include the sizes suggested (FIG. 2-8). Altering widths is easy and heights can be varied, but in the other direction you have to arrange for the parts to fit into each other.

Hardwood, finishing not less than 7/8 inch thick, is advised. This is not a project suitable for softwood. The tables have to fit into each other, and the only rails are at the back, so strong wood and good joints are essential.

Widths will have to be made by gluing boards together, and you could join random pieces. Prepare sufficient glued-up pieces before starting construction. Some work may be done on all tables at one time, but you may find it best to make all the parts of the large table first, then get sizes for the next one from it and sizes for the small one from that, so any minor variations are taken care of and you will finish with a carefully fitted unit.

Note that the legs slope (FIG. 2-8A) and the rails are arranged so in the nested tables their heights match: lower rails are the same level and the top rails vary in depth so lower edges are also level (FIG. 2-8B). Make a fullsize drawing of the main lines of the end of the large table (FIG. 2-9A). Use this as a guide to the angles of all legs.

Using this drawing as a guide to sizes and angles, mark out the pair of large table legs. Mark the positions of the top and lower rails (FIG. 2-9B and C), also the shaping at the bottom and sides.

Mark the top edge for 3/8-inch dowels at about 3-inch intervals (FIG. 2-9D and 10A).

Cut the top rail to size (FIG. 2-8C and 10B). Prepare it and the legs for dowels (FIG. 2-9E).

The bottom rail has to go through the legs, with the tenons extended and the ends rounded (FIG. 2-9F and 10C). The tenons are 1/2-inch thick (FIG. 2-9G) and the curved ends may project about 3/8 inch. Use your full-size drawing to get the angles and lengths of both rails, so the tips of the feet will finish directly under the edge of the top.

Put 7/8-inch square strips across near the tops of the legs to support the next table (FIG. 2-9H and 10D). Allow for the second top being 1/4-inch below the first one. Round down the upper edge of each piece (FIG. 2-9J) so as you slide in the table, it will lift its feet clear of the floor.

Make the top to overhang 3 inches at the ends and 1 inch back and front. The edges may be left square or you can round or mold the top angles. Leave the lower edges sharp, except for light sanding. This may not matter on the large table, but it should match the others, which need the full width to the edge for support when nesting.

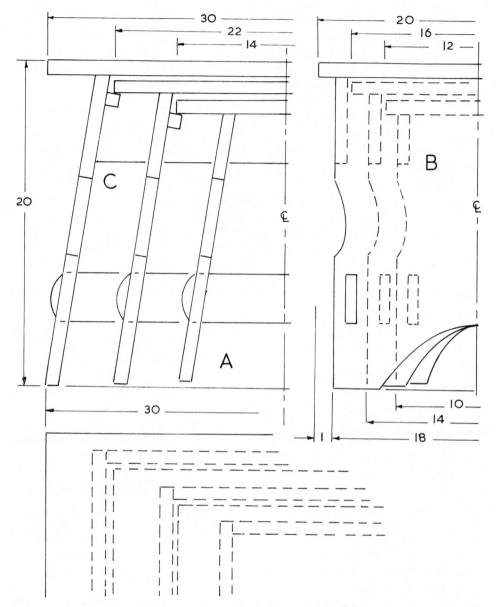

Fig. 2-8. Sizes of the three nesting tables.

When you assemble, lightly taper the ends of the dowels going upwards into the top to allow for the slopes. It should be sufficient to glue only between the rail and the top.

The second table is made in the same way. The top should fit in with ¼ inch clearance at the back and sides. Make sure the bottom rails are level, and the lower

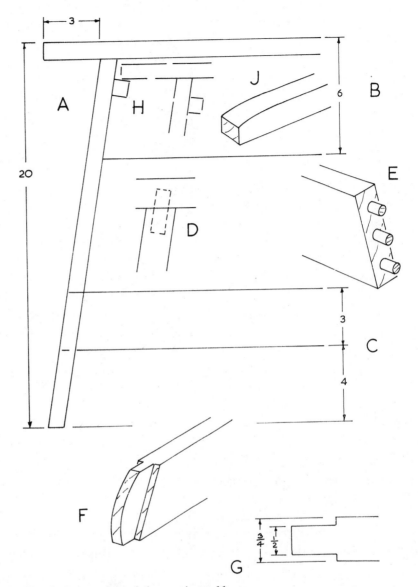

Fig. 2-9. *Details of construction of the nesting tables.*

edge of the top rail will come level with the outer one. Keep the leg slopes parallel with the large table.

The small table is shown with back rails arranged the same as the other tables. That may be satisfactory, but if you expect the small table to be used as a seat or a stool for standing on, it would be advisable to fit rails at the front as well. You can do this to the small table only because it doesn't need space for anything inside.

Treat it with a clear finish, preferably stain-resistant.

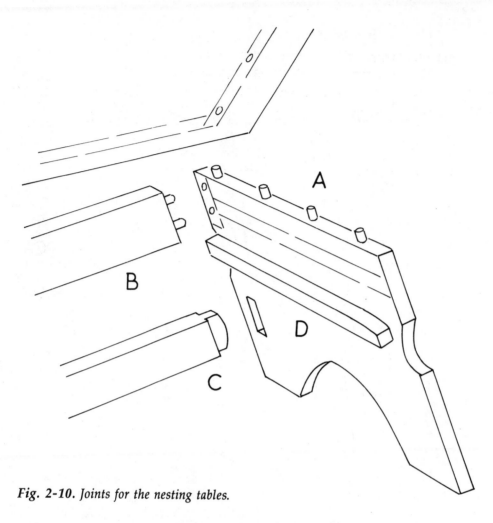

Fig. 2-10. Joints for the nesting tables.

Materials List for Nesting Tables

Large table	
1 top	$7/8 \times 20 \times 32$
2 legs	$7/8 \times 18 \times 21$
1 rail	$7/8 \times 5 1/8 \times 27$
1 rail	$7/8 \times 3 \times 32$
2 strips	$7/8 \times 7/8 \times 19$

Second table

1 top	$7/8 \times 16 \times 24$
2 legs	$7/8 \times 14 \times 20$
1 rail	$7/8 \times 4 1/4 \times 17$
1 rail	$7/8 \times 3 \times 24$
2 strips	$7/8 \times 7/8 \times 16$

Small table

1 top	$7/8 \times 12 \times 16$
2 legs	$7/8 \times 10 \times 19$
1 rail	$7/8 \times 3 \times 12$
1 rail	$7/8 \times 3 \times 16$
2 strips	$7/8 \times 7/8 \times 12$

COMPACT DINING TABLE

You may not always need a full-size dining table. If one or two of you want a quick snack or light breakfast in the kitchen, quite a small table will be all you need. There may be an alcove or a corner by a room divider where such a table and a couple of chairs would be useful. This table (FIG. 2-11) is intended to fill that need. It may have other uses in the home and could be taken onto a deck or patio, but it is designed with central pillar supports at the ends so getting in and out from stools or chairs is easy.

The whole table could be made of a good hardwood and given a polished finish, but the sizes are intended to suit stock sections of softwood under a softwood or veneered particleboard top. The wood could be painted to make an attractive table with a grained plastic veneered top.

Sizes are not critical and you may find a standard size veneered particleboard or plywood top that can be used and other sizes adapted.

The best joints for the underframing are mortise and tenon, although you could use hardwood dowels. Good joints and good glue should produce a strong table. Make the two matching end assemblies first, then join them with the lengthwise parts and finally add the top.

Make the top and bottom crosspieces (FIG. 2-12A and B), which have the same

Fig. 2-11. A compact dining table.

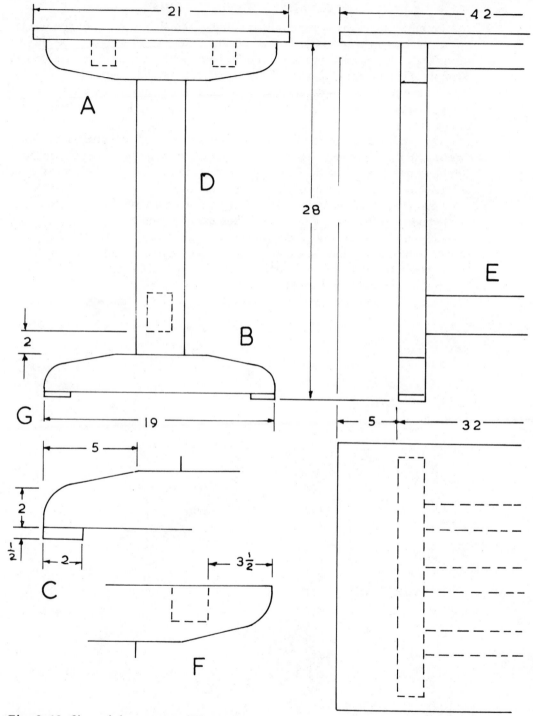

Fig. 2-12. Sizes of the compact dining table.

outlines. Mark out the pieces, including the sloping ends (FIG. 2-12C), but leave shaping until after the mortises have been cut or the dowel holes drilled.

Mark out the two posts (FIG. 2-12D and 2-14A), including double tenons at the ends (FIG. 2-13A) 1½ inches long and one-third the thickness of the wood. Mark the location of the footrail (FIG. 2-12E and 2-14B).

If dowels are to be used, allow for three ¾-inch diameter in the 4-inch post (FIG. 2-13B) and two in the 3-inch rail (FIG. 2-13C).

Mark the top crosspieces with positions for two lengthwise strips (FIG. 2-12F and 2-14C), which will be cut down to half thickness and notched in (FIG. 2-13D).

Mark and cut the lengthwise top pieces and the footrail.

Cut all the joints between these matching parts.

Complete the cutting of outlines. Put square feet under the ends of the bottom crosspieces (FIG. 2-12G and 2-14D).

Make up the end assemblies and see that they match and are square. Take sharpness off exposed edges.

When you join the ends with the lengthwise pieces, draw the footrail joints as tight as possible. You can drive a screw down through each top joint (FIG. 2-13E).

Check squareness in all directions by comparing diagonals.

Cut the top to size. Use iron-on edging strip where necessary.

Prepare the top surfaces of the framework for joining to the top with dowels. See that surfaces will meet closely without wobble. Drill for dowels (FIG. 2-14E). Dowels ⅝-inch or ¾-inch diameter at about 6-inch intervals should be sufficient.

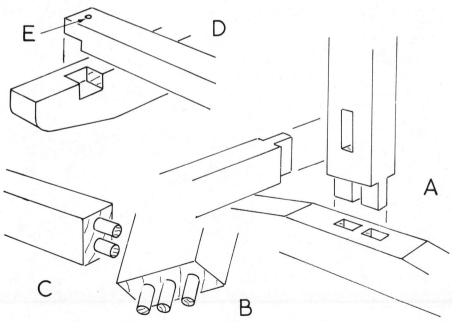

Fig. 2-13. Alternative joints for the compact dining table.

Arrange the dowels to project into the top as deeply as possible. Mark the underside of the top to match the framework, then assemble the parts while inverted.

Give the framework several coats of paint. If the top is wood-veneered, give it a clear finish, but if it is plastic veneer it will not need any treatment.

Materials List for Compact Dining Table

2 pillars	$2 \times 4 \times 28$
4 crosspieces	$2 \times 3 \times 21$
1 footrail	$2 \times 3 \times 33$
2 strips	$2 \times 2 \times 33$
1 top	$21 \times 42 \times \frac{3}{4}$ veneered particleboard

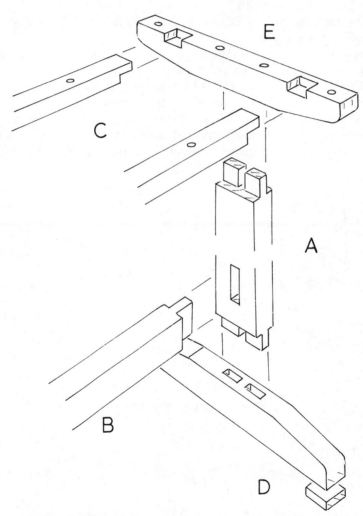

Fig. 2-14. Fitting the parts of the compact dining table together.

LIGHT FOLDING TABLE

A table which can be stored compactly, yet is easily opened, may be used for games, occasional meals at home, or taken on camping trips and brought into use any time you need extra table space. This folding table (FIG. 2-15) is not intended for heavy use, but it may be used for writing on, refreshments, or lighter hobbies. In use it has a top 25 inches by 34 inches at the usual table height. When folded it keeps its top size, but the legs fold inwards to reduce the thickness to less than 4

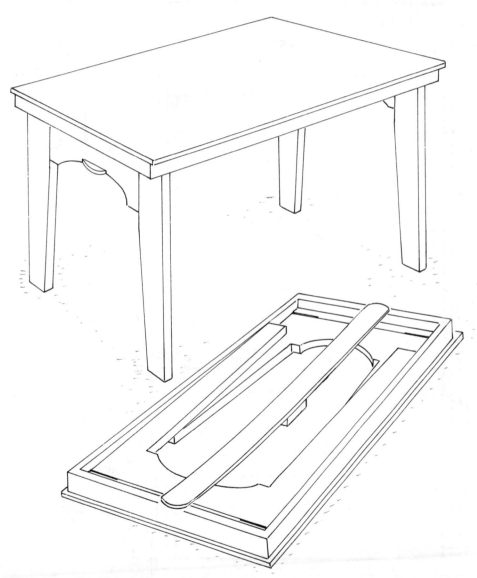

Fig. 2-15. This light folding table has a spring action to hold it erected or folded.

inches. There are no loose parts and nothing to turn or adjust to put the legs into either position—they are held by a wood spring.

Sizes are suggested (FIG. 2-16). If you alter sizes you must allow for the legs folding inwards with a few inches of length to spare, so they overlap easily.

The top may be a piece of plywood. Veneered particleboard could be used,

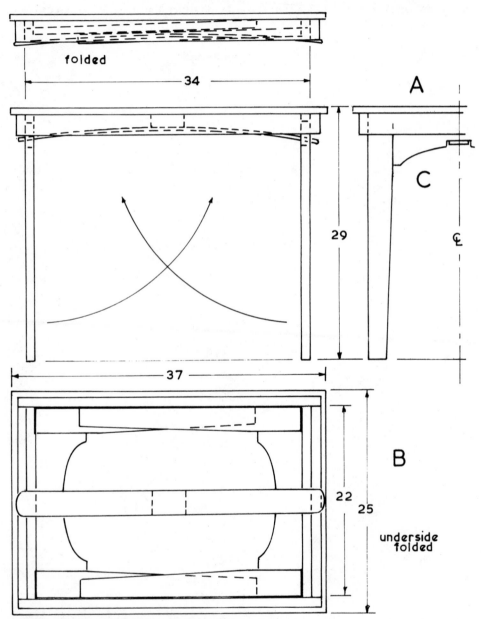

Fig. 2-16. Sizes of the light folding table.

but that would add considerably to the weight. Softwood plywood should be satisfactory. Most of the framework could also be softwood, for lightness. The spring might be straightgrained softwood, although a flexible hardwood, such as ash, would be preferable. For most purposes the finish could be paint, but for regular indoor use you may prefer to make the table of hardwood and give it a polished finish.

It will be best to make the table in three stages: the framed top, the leg assemblies and the spring. You can then ensure good fits as the units are made in turn.

Make the top like a shallow box (FIG. 2-16A and 2-17A). The sides and ends

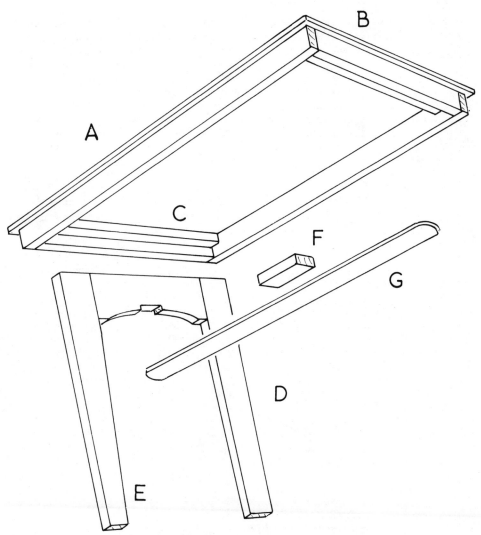

Fig. 2-17. Parts of the light folding table.

could be overlapped and glued and screwed (FIG. 2-17B), or you may wish to use dovetails or one of the other corner joints.

Cut the plywood top to overlap the framing ½ inch all around (FIG. 2-16B). Round the edges and corners (FIG. 2-18A). Assemble these parts with glue and pins or screws.

Put 1-inch square strips across inside the ends (FIG. 2-17C and 2-18B). These pieces should be the same thickness as the wood you will use for the legs, to ensure a close fit and rigidity.

That completes the top. Remove excess glue and sand all over.

The two leg assemblies are the same (FIG. 2-16C and 2-17D) and have to fit easily into the top. Construction is shown with dowels, but you could use mortise and tenon joints.

Make the four legs. They taper from 3 inches wide below where the crosspiece comes to 2 inches wide at the bottom (FIG. 2-17E). Leave some extra length at the top to be leveled after assembly.

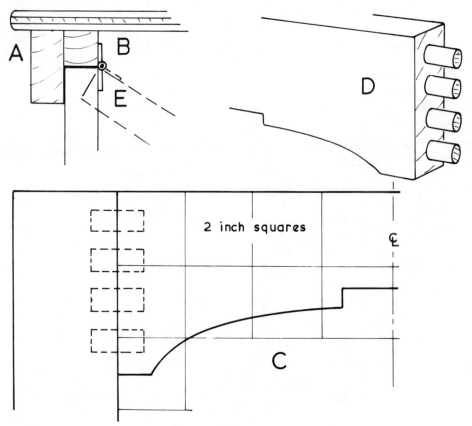

Fig. 2-18. Leg hinging and rail details for the light folding table.

Cut the crosspieces to shape (FIG. 2-18C). Squareness at the ends is important, to keep the legs parallel.

Prepare both parts of each joint for dowels — four ½-inch or ⅝-inch are shown (FIG. 2-18D).

When you join the leg assemblies, fit them inside the top to check that they are parallel and match each other.

Make a trial assembly. Use a 3-inch hinge at the top of each leg. Put it inside the leg (FIG. 2-18E), so when the leg is in the upright position it is resting against the square block and the outside framing of the top so the load will not be taken only by the hinge and its screws.

You may have to experiment with the spring, depending on the flexibility of the chosen wood. Make a block 6 inches long and 1½ inches thick (FIG. 2-17F). Join it securely to the center of the top with glue and screws.

The spring (FIG. 2-17G) has to be screwed to this block so its ends will fit easily in the leg crosspiece slots, and its springiness will hold the legs square to the top in the erected position. When folded, the spring rests over the flattened legs and its ends come on the end frame pieces of the top.

The suggested section of the spring is ½ inch by 3 inches; although it may keep this section at the center, you will probably have to thin it towards the ends. Much depends on the springiness of the wood. A piece of softwood may function with its full ½-inch thickness for the whole length, but a rather stiff piece of hardwood may have to be tapered to ¼-inch thick towards its ends.

The spring has to be forced to a curve as it is screwed down to the central block. If the pressure is too much you may reduce it by adding a packing between the spring and the block.

As you experiment with the spring you will see that it will bed down better in the crosspiece grooves if you bevel them to match its angle. When you are satisfied with the spring action, round the edges and ends of the spring and screw it to the block. Do not use glue in case you have to remove the spring for later adjustment. It will probably be sufficient to use four screws — two near each end of the block with large washers under their heads to spread the pressure.

You may wish to disassemble the table for convenience in finishing with paint or polish.

Materials List for Light Folding Table

1 top	25 × 37 × ½ plywood
2 frames	1 × 2½ × 38
2 frames	1 × 2½ × 26
2 strips	1 × 1 × 24
4 legs	1 × 3 × 30
2 legs	1 × 3 × 30
2 crosspieces	1 × 5 × 18
1 block	1½ × 3 × 8
1 spring	½ × 3 × 38

HALL TABLE

There is often not much space in an entrance hall, yet there may be a need for a table — of adequate yet economical size, so as not to limit passage. This hall table (FIG. 2-19) is, in effect, half an octagonal table with its cut side against the wall. It has an upper shelf with a back that holds the table far enough from the wall for the legs to clear any wall baseboard. A lower shelf rests on the bottom rails.

With the suggested sizes (FIG. 2-20) the table is 30 inches wide and extends 16 inches from the wall at the usual table height. It would be best to use a good hardwood. You may wish to match existing furniture. It may be preferable to have solid wood throughout, with pieces joined to make the top, but you might choose to make the top of veneered particleboard with solid edging.

Fig. 2-19. This hall table fits against the wall and takes up minimum space.

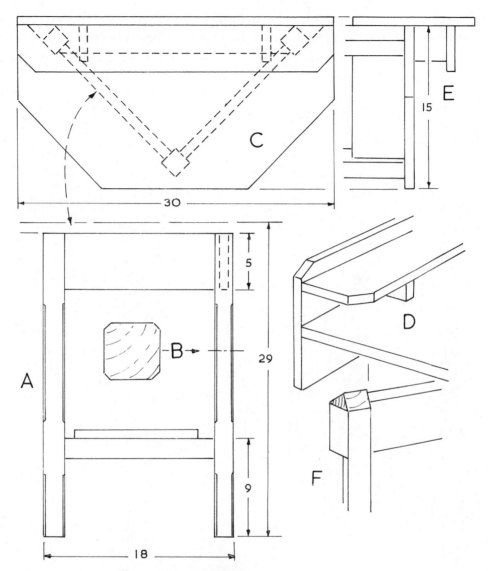

Fig. 2-20. Suggested sizes for the hall table.

Construction is not as complicated as might seem at first, since the under-framing is the same as a square table, without the fourth leg and rails connected to it. The top fits diagonally on this. The back extends behind the legs and provides the stiffness of a rear top rail. The lower shelf provides stiffness at that level.

You can make the table as two units: the legs and their framing, then the top assembly to attach to them. If you want to vary the size much, it would be advisable to set out the top first, so as to get the positions of the legs and the lengths of their rails.

Mark out the three legs (FIG. 2-20A and 2-21A) with the positions of the rails and a little excess length left at the top until after the joints have been cut. You could turn the legs between and below the rails, but it is suggested you follow the

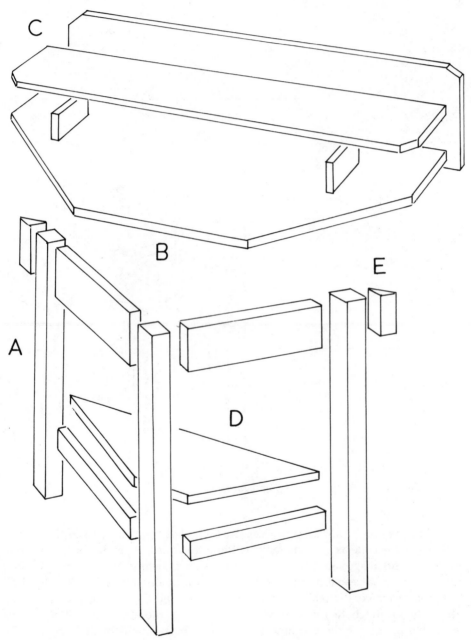

Fig. 2-21. The parts of a hall table.

general 45° theme of the table parts with small chamfers (FIG. 2-20B), leaving the rail areas square.

Decide on rail joints. You could use tenons (FIG. 2-22A and B) or dowels (FIG. 2-22C and D). Allow for the tenons or dowels projecting about 1 inch and miter the meeting corners in the front leg.

Cut the rails to length so the assembly will finish with the legs 18 inches across their outsides.

Plow grooves inside the top rails to engage with buttons when attaching the top (FIG. 2-22E). Grooves ⅜-inch wide and deep and ⅜ inch from the edge would be suitable.

Join the legs and rails together. See that each side is square, the parts are square with each other when viewed from above, and the legs stand level.

Join boards to make up the width of the top (FIG. 2-20C and 2-21B).

To mark the outline, have a shape 15 inches × 30 inches with square corners. Measure the length of a line from a corner to the center of the opposite side (FIG.

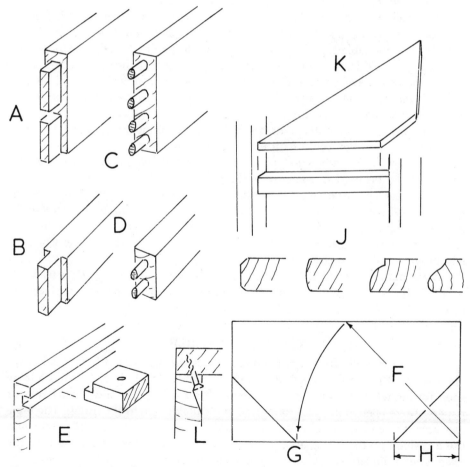

Fig. 2-22. Alternative joints and details of the top for the hall table.

Materials List for Hall Table

3 legs	$1\frac{3}{4} \times 1\frac{3}{4} \times 30$
2 rails	$1 \times 5 \times 18$
2 rails	$1 \times 2 \times 18$
1 shelf	$\frac{3}{4} \times 12 \times 24$
2 blocks	$1\frac{3}{4} \times 1\frac{3}{4} \times 7$
1 top	$1 \times 15 \times 32$
1 back	$\frac{3}{4} \times 12 \times 32$
1 shelf	$\frac{3}{4} \times 4 \times 32$
2 supports	$\frac{3}{4} \times 4 \times 5$
buttons from	$\frac{3}{4} \times 2 \times 12$

2-22F). Mark this line along the outer edge from each corner (FIG. 2-22G). Transfer this distance down the short sides (FIG. 2-22H) and join the marks. Cut this outline.

Leave the rear edge square. You could leave the other edges square or round or mold them. Some sections are suggested (FIG. 2-22J).

The back and its shelf (FIG. 2-20D and E and 2-21C) fit over the edge of the tabletop, with two supports under the shelf. The shelf could be molded in the same way as the table top. Prepare these parts for joining together with dowels, although you could use screws through the back, as their heads will be hidden against the wall. Bevel corners at 45°, or round them if you wish. Join the shelf to the back and have the supports ready, but leave joining to the table top until that has been attached to the rails.

Make the lower shelf (FIG. 2-21D and 2-22K) to rest on the lower rails. It will hold these parts square. You could fix it with counterbored screws driven downwards, and the holes filled with wood plugs, or you could use pocket screws driven upwards from below (FIG. 2-22L), so nothing shows on top.

Invert the leg assembly on the underside of the top. Have the corners of the rear legs level with the rear edge of the top. See that the assembly is central in the length. It should be sufficient to use two buttons in each rail, with the forward ones near the front leg and the others a short distance from the rear legs. The back will provide additional strength.

Make triangular fillers (2-20F) to go behind the legs and as deep as the back will overhang (FIG. 2-21E). Glue and pin these to the legs and see that rear surfaces are level.

TELEPHONE TABLE

A table especially for the telephone ensures the instrument having a known place where it is possible to sit while conversing. This table (FIG. 2-23) has a large shelf for the telephone and space underneath for directories and other books or papers. There is enough space alongside at a suitable height for sitting. The table legs are set in enough to clear the baseboard if it is put against a wall. You could use a cushion on the sitting area. Although the drawings are for a table with the telephone to the left as you face it, you could reverse the design if that would be more convenient for your situation or needs.

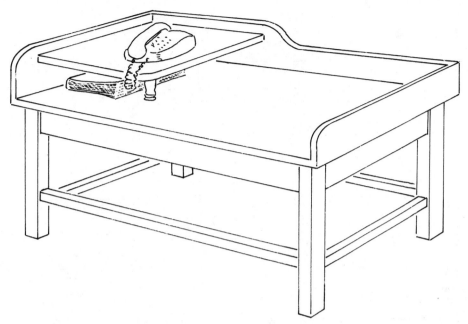

Fig. 2-23. This telephone table has space for directories and room to sit.

All parts may be solid wood, with the shelf and tabletop made by gluing boards together. Alternatively, those parts could be veneered particleboard. Rail joints are preferably mortise and tenon, although you could use dowels in the top rails. Joints for other parts are indicated in the instructions.

The sizes suggested (FIG. 2-24) should be followed, unless you need to adapt the table to fit a particular position. If you want to include an answering machine or some other equipment, it should be possible to modify sizes as necessary.

Construction can be tackled in two main assemblies. The top and all that goes above it may be treated as one unit, then the legs and rails may be made as a framework separately.

Cut the top (FIG. 2-24A and 2-26A) to size. Use this as a guide to the measurements of parts that fit against it.

Decide on the corner joints to be used for the top border strips. If you have a suitable router cutter and jig, you could use half-blind dovetails (FIG. 2-25A). You could handcut dovetails or merely lap the boards with screws from the back.

Cut the back to shape (FIG. 2-25B and 2-26B). It will fit level with the edge of the top (FIG. 2-24B).

Make the two ends (FIG. 2-26C and D) which also fit over and level with the edges of the top. Mark the shelf position on the high end and the back. Round the front corners of the ends.

Cut the shelf (FIG. 2-24C and 2-25C). Mark it and the border pieces for dowels. You could use ⅜-inch dowels at about 3 inch intervals.

The outer corner of the shelf needs support by a pillar. A turned piece (FIG.

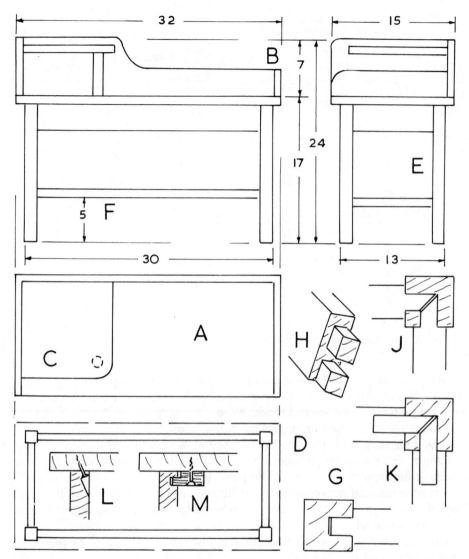

Fig. 2-24. Suggested sizes for the telephone table and alternative methods of construction.

2-25D) is suggested, with ½-inch dowels turned on their ends to fit into holes in the shelf and tabletop. If you do not have turning facilities, you could use a 1 inch square or round piece with dowels inserted in its ends. Use the shelf height marked on the border pieces as a guide to the height of the pillar. Drill the shelf and tabletop to suit.

Assemble the border to the tabletop with screws driven upwards from below, without glue. If you are using veneered particleboard there will be no problem of expansion and contraction, but with a solid wood top you must allow for the width

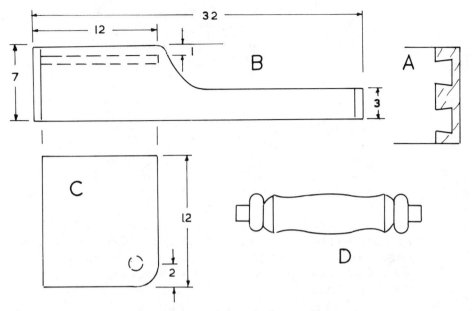

Fig. 2-25. Shapes and sizes of parts of the telephone table.

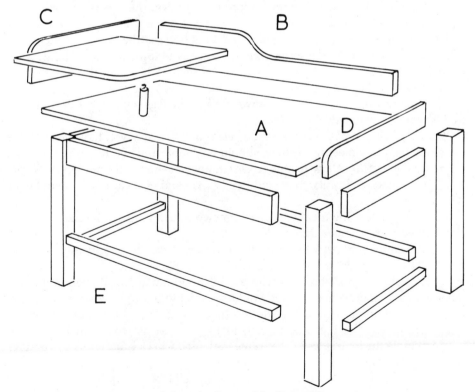

Fig. 2-26. How the parts of the telephone table fit together.

Materials List for Telephone Table

1 top	$3/4 \times$	15×34
1 back	$3/4 \times$	7×34
1 end	$3/4 \times$	7×17
1 end	$3/4 \times$	3×17
1 shelf	$3/4 \times$	12×12
4 legs	$1\frac{1}{2} \times 1\frac{1}{2} \times$	18
2 rails	$1 \times$	3×30
2 rails	$1 \times$	3×13
2 rails	$1 \times$	1×30
2 rails	$1 \times$	1×13
1 pillar	$1 \times$	1×7

altering slightly. If the table will be used in a centrally heated room, it will help to store the wood for the top for a few weeks in the same conditions, if you can spare the time, so the wood's moisture content will stabilize to suit the atmosphere. With particleboard, drill holes that are a fairly close fit on the screws, which may be #8 gauge by $1\frac{1}{2}$ inch. With solid wood, drill for a close fit along the back, but use oversize holes across the ends, to allow for a little movement.

Join the back corners and then the shelf, before screwing to the table top.

Arrange the leg and rail framework so the size over the legs is 1 inch in from the edges of the top (FIG. 2-24D).

Mark out the legs (FIG. 2-24E and 2-26E) to give a seat height of 17 inches, or whatever you prefer. Leave some excess wood at the tops until after joints have been cut. The front lower rails (FIG. 2-24F) are 1 inch higher than the side rails, so the mortises are kept apart for stronger joints.

It would be unwise to join the lower rails to the legs with single dowels, and they should be tenoned (FIG. 2-24G).

The top rails may be tenoned or doweled. In both cases you have to allow for the joints each way meeting. Tenons should be double and cut down from the top of the leg (FIG. 2-24H). Allow for the tenons almost meeting with mitered ends (FIG. 2-24J). If you choose dowels, they could be $1/2$ inch and also cut with mitered ends (FIG. 2-24K).

The rails determine the size of the framework. Cut them so the sizes over the legs will be correct under the tabletop.

If the tabletop is particleboard, you can use pocket screws in the rails (FIG. 2-24L). Pockets may be cut with a chisel or with a Forstner bit.

You could use pocket screws with a solid wood top and drill oversized screw holes to allow for movement, but it would be better to plow grooves inside the top rails and use buttons screwed to the top (FIG. 2-24M). With both methods, space attachments two at each end and others along the sides at about 6-inch intervals.

Assemble the long sides of the framework first. Check squareness by comparing diagonals and see that opposite sides match.

Join these parts with the short rails and again check squareness. Test the shape under the top.

Make a trial assembly of the two units, then take them apart for convenience in sanding and applying a finish.

The two units need not be finished in the same way. A darker lower framework could go under a lighter or natural finish top.

OVAL GARDEN TABLE AND BENCHES

We are all familiar with the rectangular picnic table with its seats attached to the legs and with tables with independent benches, otherwise similar in general pattern. For our own outdoor furniture, most of us prefer something more individualistic that differs from the conventional type. Tables with shaped outlines do not lend themselves to quantity production, and matching benches require even more individual attention. This outdoor table with matching benches (FIG. 2-27) is certainly different from the usual furniture you may see in neighbors' and friends' yards.

There is obviously more work to achieve satisfactory results with shaped furniture; but although the increased work requires care, there is none of the precision woodworking that you would expect with indoor cabinetry. The table could be accompanied by just a pair of side benches, or you might complete the set

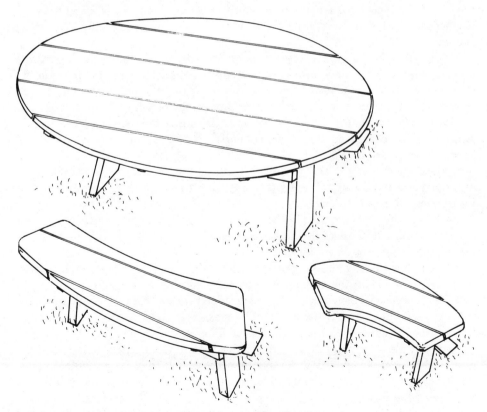

Fig. 2-27. An oval garden table with matching benches.

with two end benches. Although construction is simple, the amount of work may be too much for one weekend, and you may wish to make the table as one project, then deal with the benches at other times.

The sizes suggested are for a tabletop 48 inches by 72 inches and benches which match the curves and are 16 inches wide on their curves. You could work to other sizes, but would have to start with an ellipse the size of the table. Heights are 30 inches for the table and 18 inches for the benches, which should suit most situations on soft ground or a hard deck or patio.

The main parts of the framework are 2-inch × 4-inch sections. Tops are 1½ inch thick and widths of boards have to be arranged as advised in the drawings and instructions. You could use softwood treated with preservative, but it would be better to use a weather-resistant hardwood. Parts are joined with screws, preferably brass or other damp-resistant metal, or steel protected by plating or galvanizing. You could also use waterproof glue in the joints. The tops of the table and benches are not closely-joined boards. It is better to leave gaps of about ¼ inch for drainage of rainwater if the furniture is left outside in bad weather.

Start by laying out one-quarter of the tops of table and benches full-size (FIG. 2-28), preferably on a piece of plywood or hardboard. One corner of the sheet will then serve as the centerlines. The grid of 6 inch squares will provide a guide. Draw the elliptical tabletop. When you are satisfied with this shape, draw the outsides of the benches 16 inches from and parallel to it. Cut off the ends of the benches as shown.

You can make the tops of any number of boards, but it is advisable to arrange them so the underframing comes close to support thinly tapered board ends. As shown, the tabletop is made of five boards finishing a little under 10 inches wide (FIG. 2-28A). When you arrange the board widths on the benches, there should be at least 4 inches left at the narrowest points of the inner boards (FIG. 2-28B and C). Arrange outer boards so their tapered ends do not extend very far past the supports (FIG. 2-28D and E).

Arrange a crossbar to extend the full width of the top near each end (FIG. 2-28F and 2-30A) and another at the center (FIG. 2-28G and 2-30B). The tops of the legs come inside the end crossbars.

Arrange the seat crossbars in the same way (FIG. 2-28H and J and 2-30C). There should be enough stiffness in the bench tops, but if necessary, you could put a crossbar at the center of a long bench.

From your full-size drawing mark out the lengths of the crossbars, but leave some excess wood on the ends to be trimmed later.

The legs across in sawbuck manner, arranged with a slightly greater spread at the feet than at the top. Lay them out full-size as shown (FIG. 2-29A and B). From the top crossbar lengths, obtained from the tabletop drawing, mark in the distance shown. Cut the legs with tightly-fitting halved joints where they cross (FIG. 2-30D and E). Do not cut away any more than is necessary. If they do not enter exactly level, projection of up to ½ inch is stronger than cutting away too much and weakening the legs.

Glue and screw the legs parts and see that opposite pairs match. Glue and

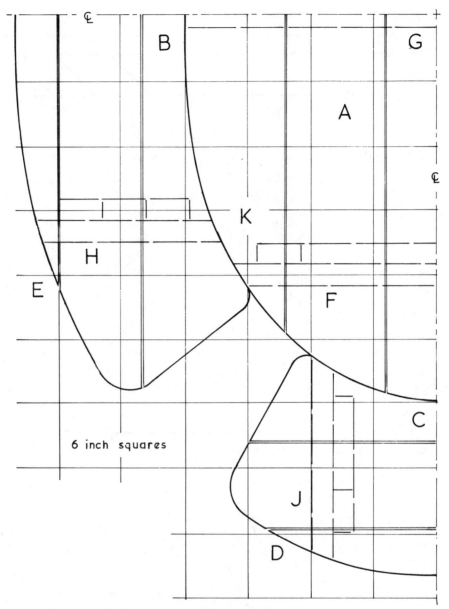

Fig. 2-28. Shapes of the oval garden table top and benches.

screw the legs to their crossbars, and again check that those that are paired will match.

Link the pairs of legs for the table with rails (FIG. 2-29C and 2-30F). Have the legs standing on a flat surface and see that they are upright when you glue and screw on the rails. Measure between the ends to see that they are parallel.

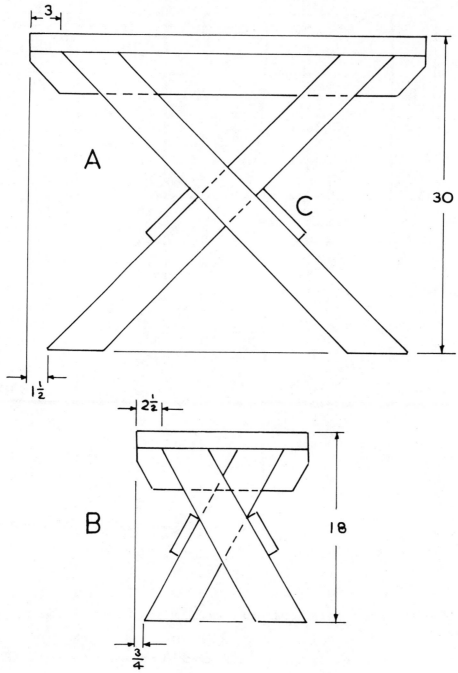

Fig. 2-29. Leg arrangements for the oval garden table and benches.

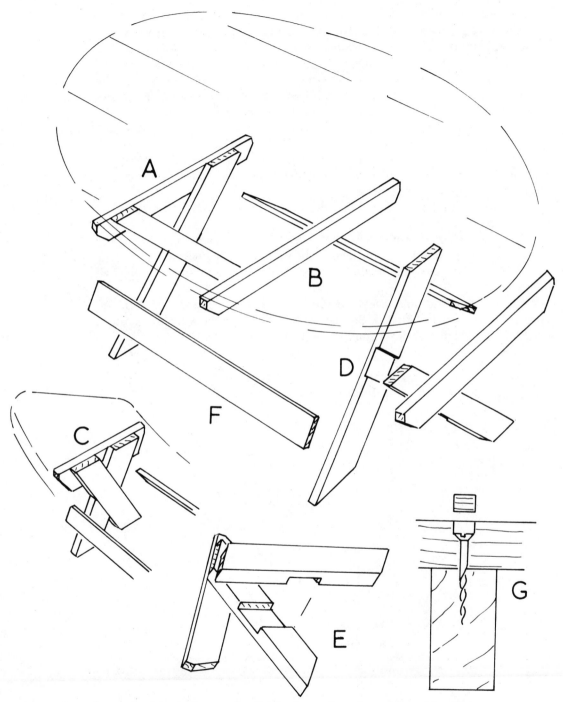

Fig. 2-30. Fitting together the legs and rails for the oval garden table and benches.

Use your full-size drawing as a guide for cutting the boards for the top. It will be helpful if you make a paper or hardboard template of the quarter curve, so you get the top symmetrical. Leave finishing the edges to the exact curves until after assembly, so you can allow for slight variations and get a fair curve all around.

With the boards inverted in the pattern you prefer, mark the positions of the crossbars and drill for screws. Have at least two holes at each crossing of a board. Screws should be long and stout—#12 gauge by 3 inch may be suitable.

Counterbore the holes on top so you can glue in plugs after assembly (FIG. 2-30G).

Assemble the top to its supports with glue and screws. Add the central crossbar. Trim the ends of all crossbars at the same time you trim the curved outline and bevel them underneath.

Take off any sharpness around the edges of the top and anywhere exposed on the legs and framing.

Follow a similar procedure with the seats. Arrange the spacing between the legs so they will permit the side benches to be pushed partly under the table (FIG. 2-28K) when out of use. Round the corners of the seats and smooth edges all around.

Apply a finish to suit the wood. Some durable hardwoods are best left untreated. Others may be oiled. Softwood should be treated with preservative, which may be followed with a compatible paint.

Materials List for Oval Garden Table and Benches

Table

4 legs	$2 \times 4 \times 48$
2 crossbars	$2 \times 4 \times 42$
1 crossbar	$2 \times 4 \times 50$
2 rails	$1 \times 6 \times 50$
1 top	$1\frac{1}{2} \times 10 \times 74$
2 tops	$1\frac{1}{2} \times 10 \times 72$
2 tops	$1\frac{1}{2} \times 10 \times 62$

Side Benches

8 legs	$2 \times 4 \times 24$
4 crossbars	$2 \times 4 \times 20$
4 rails	$1 \times 3 \times 42$
2 tops	$1\frac{1}{2} \times 8 \times 72$
2 tops	$1\frac{1}{2} \times 10 \times 72$
2 tops	$1\frac{1}{2} \times 5 \times 52$

End Benches

8 legs	$2 \times 4 \times 24$
4 crossbars	$2 \times 4 \times 20$
4 rails	$1 \times 3 \times 24$
2 tops	$1\frac{1}{2} \times 8 \times 44$
2 tops	$1\frac{1}{2} \times 8 \times 40$
2 tops	$1\frac{1}{2} \times 5 \times 40$

3

Seating

The human body is not meant to stand erect all the time, so we need seats. Their variety is considerable and much seating is too advanced to be considered weekend working projects. However, there are many forms of seating which are easy to make and economical in terms of working time.

Stools and benches are simple and effective seats. They do not have backs, but there are many occasions when a person does not require that degree of relaxation or support. Chairs, either for sitting at a table or for relaxing, have advanced designs that may not be within the reach of a weekend woodworker, but there are still some simpler versions.

Your individually-made seating may be tailored to a particular position or situation, or may include a secondary function such as storage. If someone needs a seat higher or lower, wider or narrower, you can make it to suit.

Outdoor furniture can be constructed differently than quantity produced examples. Seating you make should not represent attempts to copy manufactured furniture; instead, you have the opportunity to express your individuality in something made to suit your situation and needs.

TWO-PART STOOL

Stools are useful in many parts of the home, but particularly in the kitchen, where the cook will be glad to sit on a high stool or use a lower one to stand on to reach a high shelf. This stool (FIG. 3-1) offers three possible configurations. There is an upholstered seat at 26 inches from the floor, which allows working at a countertop in about the same attitude as when standing. This can be taken apart into two low stools. One has a strong top for standing on at about 13 inches from

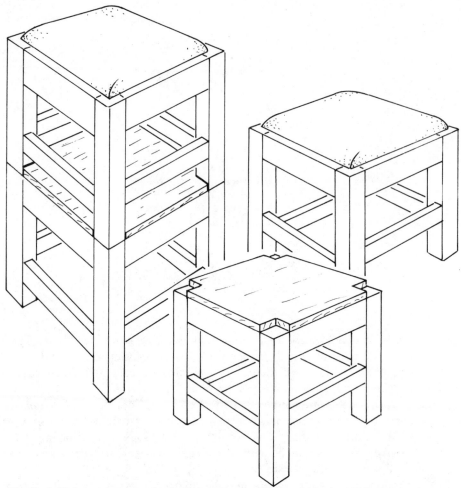

Fig. 3-1. This two-part stool may be used as a tall seat or separated into an upholstered low stool and another for standing on.

the floor. The other brings the upholstered seat down to slightly lower than chair height, which might be appreciated by a child.

The two parts of the stool are basically similar and should be made of hardwood with plywood tops. Mortise and tenon joints are suggested, but you could use ½ inch dowels, two at each place. Stools may be expected to withstand rocking and twisting loads on the joints, so they must be strong.

The sizes shown (FIG. 3-2) are for a 14 inch square seat. You could alter this, and the stool need not be square. However, for the sake of stability, do not make the stool too narrow. The instructions describe construction of one section of the stool, at first, but you may prefer to make both at the same time so all parts match.

Prepare the wood for the legs and mark them for the positions of the rails (FIG. 3-2A). Leave a little extra length at the tops until after the mortises have been cut, or

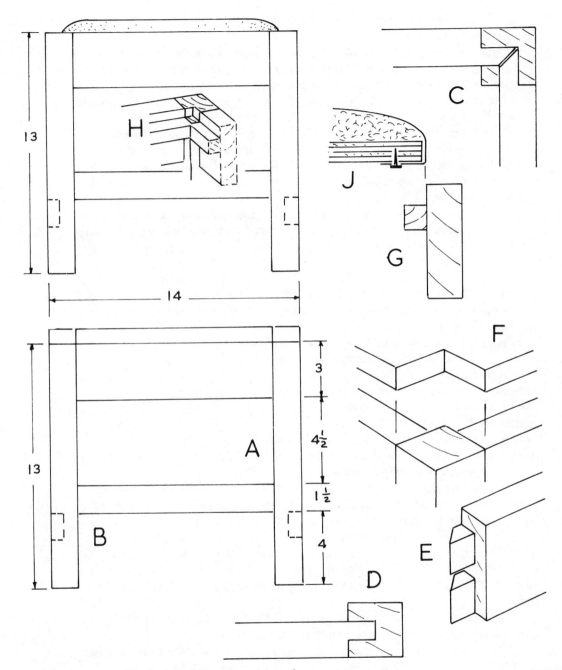

Fig. 3-2. Sizes and construction of the two-part stool.

dowel holes drilled. The legs are paired so the lower rails one way are above those the other way (FIG. 3-2B).

Mark the lengths of all rails together, if possible, so distances between shoulders (if tenoned) or ends (if doweled) are the same. If you are making the stool other than square, mark all the rails in each direction together.

The rails will finish level with the outside surfaces of the legs. Barefaced tenons ½-inch thick will fit mortises in the centers of the legs. Allow enough length on the top rail tenons to meet with a matter (FIG. 3-2C). Since lower rails are at different levels, the tenons may be cut square and a little longer (FIG. 3-2D).

Cut tenons and matched mortises for the lower rails the full depth of each rail.

The 3-inch deep top rail is better given double tenons cut down ½ inch from the top (FIG. 3-2E).

Have all the tenons and mortises cut ready. Trim the miters on the top rails so they will not quite meet when the joints are clamped, otherwise the shoulders may not pull tight. Similarly, see that the tenons on the lower rails will not quite reach the bottoms of the mortises.

Put together opposite pairs of sides and see that they are square, without twist and match each other. Clamp tightly, but you can drive fine nails from the insides of the legs through the tenons, if you have to remove clamps from any part before the glue has set.

Join with the rails the other way and check for squareness and freedom from twist. Check that the stools match when one is stood on the other.

Make the top for the lower stool (FIG. 3-1 and 3-2F). It reaches the edges of the rails, but is cut away at each corner. If you have made everything exactly to size, the two stools will match in every position, but that is unlikely and does not matter. If the upper stool rests on the lower one better in one position than another, mark two matching legs, then cut away the top so it matches the feet of the upper stool, which should make push fits in the corner notches of the top. Glue and screw the plywood top in place.

The base for the upholstered top is a piece of ½-inch plywood. To support it, put strips around inside the rails (FIG. 3-2G). At the corners, cut away the tops of the legs to continue the lines of the rails into notches (FIG. 3-2H).

The size of the plywood base for the seat will depend on the covering material used for the top, which has to wrap over the edge of the plywood and be tacked underneath (FIG. 3-2J). Allow enough clearance so the seat can be pressed in. Although it is helpful to have it removable, you do not want it so loose that it falls out.

Use plastic or rubber foam about 1-inch thick for the seat. Cut it a little oversize so its edges are compressed by the covering.

The covering may be cloth or plastic-coated fabric. If possible, choose material with some stretch in it both ways, as that is easier to fit smoothly.

Work with the seat inverted. Pull fabric on opposite edges, first at the centers of the sides. Tack underneath far enough in to be clear of the supporting strips. Work from the centers towards the corners. Spacing of tacks will depend on the

Materials List for Two-part Stool

8 legs	$1\frac{1}{2} \times 1\frac{1}{2} \times 15$
8 rails	$1 \times 3 \times 14$
8 rails	$1 \times 1\frac{1}{4} \times 14$
1 lower top	$15 \times 15 \times \frac{3}{4}$ plywood
4 supports	$\frac{5}{8} \times \frac{5}{8} \times 14$
1 upper top	$14 \times 14 \times \frac{1}{2}$ plywood

fabric, but somewhere between 1 and 2 inches should get the material to smooth curves on the top.

At each corner, cut away some of the excess material and pull the rest to overlap for tacking—it is the shaping on the top which is important. Finally trim excess cloth neatly inside the lines of tacks.

Level the outsides of the rails with the legs and sand all parts thoroughly. Take sharpness off edges of legs and rails. Bevel or round the bottoms of legs so they are less likely to mark floor coverings. Finish to suit the wood and other furniture, probably with stain and polish or varnish.

TAKE-DOWN YARD BENCH

If you live in an area where the climate is such that outdoor furniture ought to be protected under cover in the winter, it is an advantage if some of the furniture can be reduced in size for storage. Some of it may be made to fold, but it can usually be made more rigid and substantial if it is a take-down design.

This bench (FIG. 3-3A) is a strong seat for use anywhere in the yard or garden, or on a patio or deck. When you wish to reduce its size for storage, the legs and the lower rails may be taken off, leaving the top and its attached rails a total depth of about 4 inches. Assembly is with pegs in the manner used for much larger furniture in medieval castles.

The parts can be cut from 1-inch × 12-inch boards which may be softwood, but for a longer-lasting bench it would be better to use a durable type of hardwood. The suggested height and length (FIG. 3-3B) should suit most needs, but you can alter them without affecting the method of construction.

The legs are drawn sloping, which helps stability, but you could made them upright if you want simpler construction. The rails go through the legs with tusk tenons, where they are held with pegs.

Set out the main lines of one end full-size on a piece of hardboard or plywood (FIG. 3-4A). This will give you the length of the legs and the angles to cut various parts. Set an adjustable bevel to the angle and use it for marking all parts which have to match.

Make the two legs (FIG. 3-3C and 3-5A). Cut the ends to the angles on the full-size drawing. Mark the lower mortises centrally and the upper mortises 2 inches in from the edges, with outlines on both sides, so you will get the mortise angles correct.

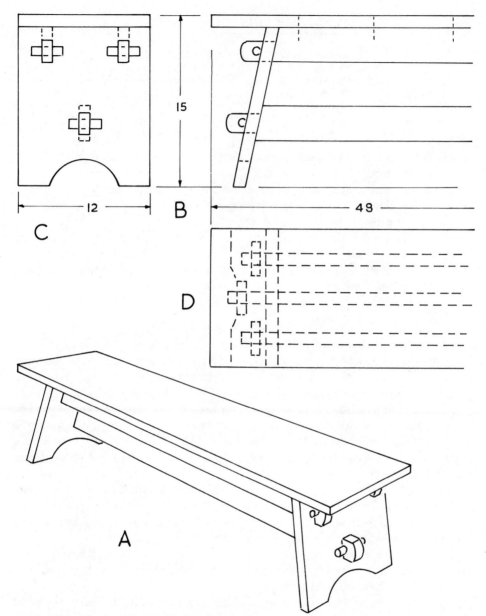

Fig. 3-3. *This yard bench may be taken apart for storage.*

Delay cutting the mortises until you have the tenons ready to match. Cut the hollows that form feet on the legs. Keep the top of the curves 2 inches from the mortises to leave ample end grain for strength.

Note how far back the rail tenons and their shoulders will come from the end of the top (FIG. 3-4B and C). Mark the rails to suit.

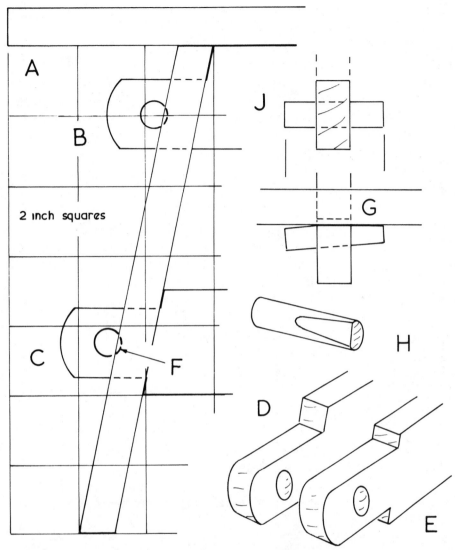

A

B

2 inch squares

C

F

J

G

H

D

E

Fig. 3-4. The shapes of parts and the method of assembly of the take-down yard bench.

All rails have 2-inch deep tenons, but the upper ones allow a 1 inch shoulder above (FIG. 3-4D and 3-5B) and the lower rail has central tenons (FIG. 3-4E and 3-5C). Cut the tenons and their matching mortises.

Make a trial assembly of the legs and three rails. See that the rail shoulders pull tight against the legs and the assembly is square and level.

Drill ¾-inch holes across the tenons so they come about ⅛ inch below the surfaces of the legs. This is to allow the pegs to pull the joints tight (FIG. 3-4F and G).

You could turn tapered pegs to lock the tenons, but it will be satisfactory to use pieces of ¾-inch hardwood dowel rod, planed to a taper (FIG. 3-4H). Cut the

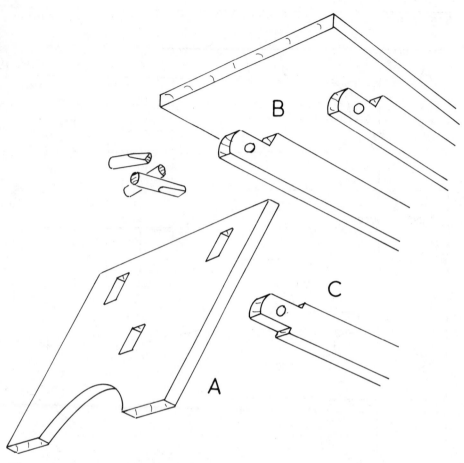

Fig. 3-5. *The parts at one end of the take-down yard bench.*

Materials List for Take-down Yard Bench

1 top	1 × 12 × 50
2 legs	1 × 12 × 16
3 rails	1 × 3 × 48
pegs from	24 × ¾ diameter

pegs too long at first, then after a trial assembly, trim them so they project 1 inch each side of their tenon (FIG. 3-4J).

The top (FIG. 3-3D) is a plain board. Lightly round the corners and edges.

Invert the lower assembly on the underside of the top and mark where the rails will come. Drill for screws in these positions — #10 gauge by 2-inch screws at 6-inch intervals are suitable. You could countersink for the screw heads on top, but the neatest finish is to counterbore and glue plugs over the screw heads, so there is no metal exposed on the top of the bench, to rust or to catch in clothing.

See that there will be clearance above the legs to allow disassembly, then screw the top to the rails. You could use waterproof glue as well.

If you have used a durable hardwood you may leave it untreated or coat it with linseed oil. Other woods may be treated with preservative or painted.

LOCKER SEAT

A long seat with storage underneath is a development of the chest, which was almost the only piece of furniture in our poorer forefathers' homes. The chest stored most of the family possessions and served as a seat. The seat is particularly suitable for putting under a window, where it may have several cushions scattered on it, or there may be one long fitted cushion or pad.

This locker seat (FIG. 3-6) has access via sliding doors at the front, so the disadvantage of having to lift a chest lid is avoided. The seat shown (FIG. 3-7) has four sliding doors. They allow access to up to half the interior at one time, either divided in parts or one complete half. If you need to get at more space, you can lift

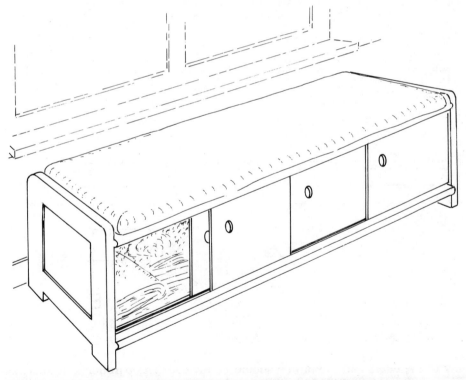

Fig. 3-6. This locker seat has sliding doors and is suitable for positioning under a window.

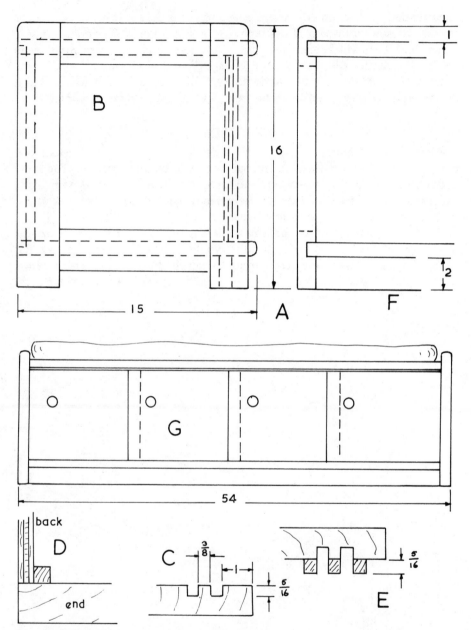

Fig. 3-7. Sizes and sections of the locker seat.

any of the doors out. The inside should be divided. The partition(s) also act as supports for the top. There may be a central one, but better support for possibly heavy and long use would be provided by two partitions, dividing the inside into three compartments, each just over 24 inches. If there is any oversize item you want to store, the divisions could be irregularly spaced.

Hardwood is advisable, although you could make a satisfactory seat with softwood. The sliding doors should be hardwood plywood in any case. The ends and partitions are shown framed, but they could be solid wood. Outside panels should be the same plywood as used for the doors. The plywood back could be any type.

The suggested height and width (FIG. 3-7A) should be a comfortable size. You may wish to alter the overall length to suit available space or the width of a window the seat is to match. The instructions and materials list are for a seat with framed ends and two partitions.

Start by making the two framed ends (FIG. 3-7B, 3-8A, and 3-9A). Groove sufficient wood to take the plywood panels (FIG. 3-8B). Allow for a panel making a push fit in its groove.

Mark out the uprights together. Leave a little extra length at the tops until after the joints have been cut. Although it may be possible to make the frames with dowel joints, it would be better to use mortise and tenon joints.

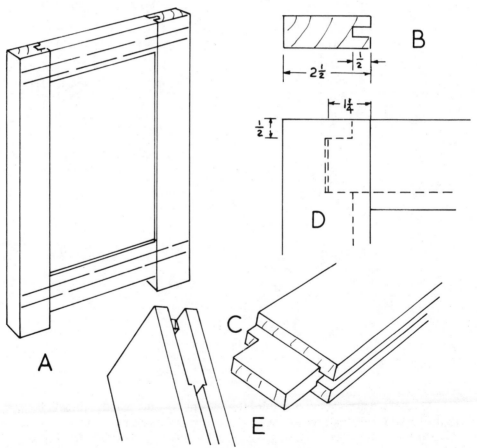

Fig. 3-8. Suggested constructional details of the locker seat ends.

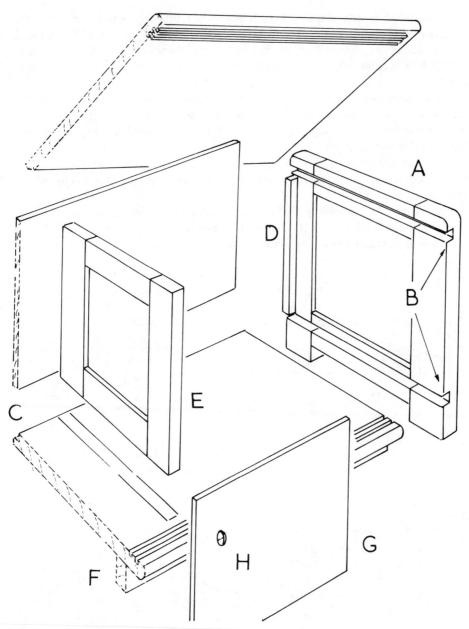

Fig. 3-9. Parts of the locker seat.

Make the tenons about one-third the thickness of the wood. This will be more than the width of the grooves. At the top corners make haunches (FIG. 3-8C) as deep as the grooves. This is unnecessary at the lower joints where the legs extend. The tenons may go about halfway through the uprights (FIG. 3-8D). Cut matching mortises and tenons (FIG. 3-8E). Let the mortises be a little too deep so the ends of the tenons do not reach them before a joint is tight on the surface.

Cut the plywood panels so they will not quite reach the bottoms of the grooves during asembly, and they cannot prevent the corner joints pulling tight. When you assemble, glue the corner joints, but a few spots of glue at widely-spaced points in the groove should be sufficient for the panels and avoid the problem of removing excess glue. See that the two finished ends match.

Glue together boards for the top and bottom, which are the same size. They should extend ½ inch forward of the ends and will be rounded, but do not round them until after doing other work on them.

There are grooves at the front of both pieces for the sliding doors. With ¼-inch hardwood plywood, make the grooves about ⁵⁄₁₆-inch wide so the doors will slide easily. Cut the grooves ⁵⁄₁₆-inch deep (FIG. 3-7C) in both parts.

Top and bottom have to fit into dado grooves across the ends (FIG. 3-9B). Take the grooves halfway through the thickness of the wood.

Rabbet the rear edges of top and bottom to take the plywood back (FIG. 3-9C).

You could rabbet the rear edges of the ends between the grooves, but it will be simpler to put strips there level with the rabbets in the other parts (FIG. 3-7D and 3-9D).

Glue and pin strips to deepen the slots in the top piece (FIG. 3-7E). Stop them at the ends to allow the wood to go into the dado grooves. These allow the doors to slide without falling out, yet it will be possible to lift them clear, as described below.

Using the ends as a guide to size, make the two partitions (FIG. 3-9E). The height is the distance between the grooves, and the width should be kept back from the strips along the top of the seat. The method of construction is the same as the ends, except the wood is thinner.

Mark the locations of the partitions on the top and bottom and prepare all parts for dowels. Once the seat is assembled there will be little load on the dowels, and it should be sufficient to use three ⅜-inch dowels in each joint.

Round the front edges of top and bottom. Round the top corners of the ends and well round the parts that will project above the seat. Do any necessary sanding of parts before assembly.

You may fit a kickboard (FIG. 3-7F and 3-9F). This will prevent sagging if the lengthwise boards seem too flexible, and will close a part where cleaning out dust would be difficult. Use a few dowels to position it.

Have the back ready, then join the partitions to top and bottom, then those parts to the ends. Glue and screw the back to hold the other parts square. If the dado joints are a good fit, they should be strong enough; but if you have doubts, drive a screw upwards diagonally in each end a few inches from the front. The back will hold the other ends of these joints. Stand the seat on a flat surface while the glue sets, to guard against the risk of twist.

The four doors (FIG. 3-7G and 3-9G) can be the same. Their widths should allow about 2-inch overlap when they are evenly spaced. When a door is raised as high as possible into the top groove, its bottom should be clear of the bottom, so it may

Materials List for Locker Seat

4 end uprights	$1\frac{1}{4} \times 2\frac{1}{2} \times 18$
4 end rails	$1\frac{1}{4} \times 2\frac{1}{2} \times 15$
2 end panels	$13 \times 13 \times \frac{1}{4}$ plywood
2 partition uprights	$1 \times 2\frac{1}{2} \times 16$
2 partition rails	$1 \times 2\frac{1}{2} \times 15$
2 partition panels	$13 \times 13 \times \frac{1}{4}$ plywood
1 top	$1 \times 15 \times 56$
1 bottom	$1 \times 15 \times 56$
1 back	$14 \times 56 \times \frac{1}{2}$ plywood
4 doors	$14 \times 16 \times \frac{1}{4}$ plywood
3 door guides	$\frac{5}{16} \times \frac{3}{8} \times 54$

be pulled out. Its weight will keep it in place for normal sliding, but you can remove any door after lifting it.

Drill a 1-inch or larger hole at a convenient height and far enough from the edge to be clear of the next overlapping door (FIG. 3-9H). Round the edges of the hole. Slightly round and sand the edges of the doors, so they slide easily. You may need to sand inside the grooves with abrasive paper wrapped around the edge of a piece of plywood. When you finish the wood, it will ease movement if you put some candle wax in the bottom grooves.

Finish the wood with stain and polish to match other furniture. Softwood may be stained, but it might be better painted.

Although it would be possible to use the seat unpadded, cushion may be used or a fitted single upholstered full-size cushion would be luxurious.

HEAVY-DUTY BENCH

In some situations outdoor seating has to be left in position for most of the year, so it has to withstand all kinds of weather, particularly rain and snow. This means it should be strong and with parts stout enough to not be weakened if thoroughly soaked. If it is in a public place, it may also have to withstand rough treatment and should be heavy enough to be difficult to move or turn over. This bench (FIG. 3-10) is made of 2-inch × 4-inch wood. It can offer reasonable comfort, but is very substantially constructed and should be able to remain serviceable, even if neglected and abused.

Wood specified as 2-inch × 4-inch section will be about ¼ inch less than that each way after planing. This is allowed for in the design. Use hardwood, if you wish, but softwood treated with preservative should be satisfactory and much cheaper. Choose wood without large knots, to limit weak parts or any tendency to warp. If possible, buy wood already treated with preservative, otherwise treat it with preservative liberally during construction, so you get it into parts that would be difficult to reach if you waited until the seat was complete.

Some parts are held with nuts, washers and bolts. These could be any bolts, ⅜-inch or ½-inch diameter, but galvanized carriage bolts are particularly suitable.

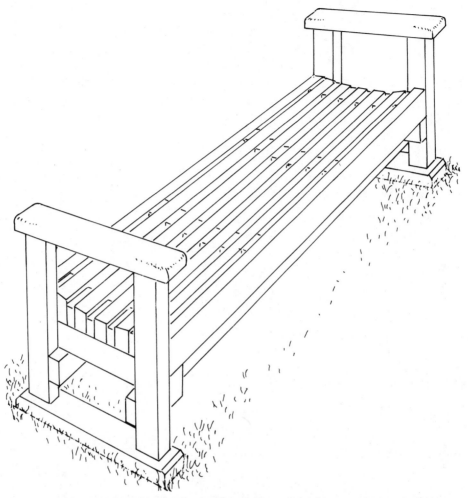

Fig. 3-10. This heavy-duty outdoor bench is intended for exposure and hard use.

You will need 2-inch and 4-inch nails. Common nails are suitable, preferably galvanized, but most of the nails will be buried, so they are less likely to be attacked by rust. It will also help to use waterproof glue in the joints if the preservative is of a type that will accept the glue.

The seat is shown with a hollowed top (FIG. 3-11A). If you have a table saw with an adjustable angle fence, the parts are easy to cut. If you are unable to shape the strips, the seat could be left with a flat top and rather less comfort. In any case, the spaces along the seat allow rainwater to drain through. A 72-inch seat is specified, but you can alter this without affecting construction.

Make the seat first. The finished thicknesses of the wood may result in a slightly different total width of the assembly, but that doesn't matter, providing their ends are made to match.

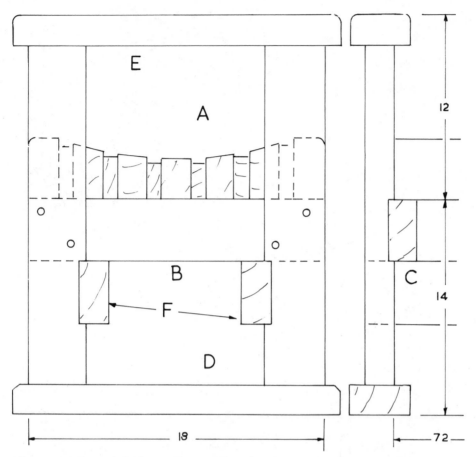

Fig. 3-11. Sizes of the heavy-duty outdoor bench.

Draw the end view of the seat (FIG. 3-12A) full-size on the edge of a piece of scrap plywood. The outside pieces are parallel. The curve dips to make the center piece 2½ inches deep, and this will show you the sizes and angles to cut the other pieces.

Prepare the strips. Plane the upper surfaces of the angled pieces. Round the edges of the outer strips. You may be able to do a little planing of the pieces after assembly, but it is easier to deal with the surfaces while the parts are separate.

Prepare spacers 1 inch thick and 4 inches long (FIG. 3-12B and C). In each space there will be a block at each end, then others at about 24 inch spacing, so if you make the seat 72 inches long there will be two more sets of blocks. The spacers need not come to the tops of the seat strips, and there is no need to bevel their top edges. Make enough blocks for the whole seat before starting assembly.

In each joint there are two nails to hold the spacer in place (FIG. 3-12D), then the next strip is held to the spacer with a nail going right through the spacer and into the strip behind (FIG. 3-12E). To reduce the risk of splitting, drill for all nails.

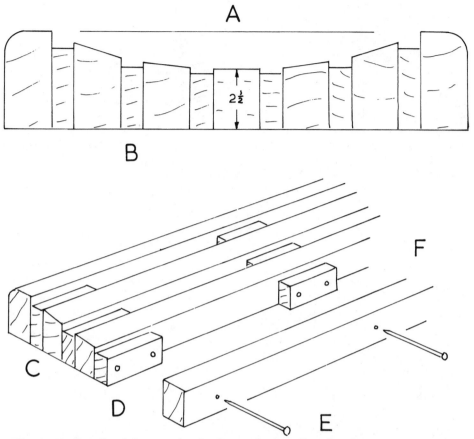

Fig. 3-12. Details of the seat for the heavy-duty outdoor bench.

Experiment in a piece of scrap wood to check what diameter undersize holes will suit the nails.

Assemble progressively across the seat, fitting spacers and strips in turn (FIG. 3-12F). Do any final trimming necessary and square across the ends of the seat.

Each end assembly consists of two legs with supporting rail for the seat (FIG. 3-11B) and top and bottom rails which make an armrest and a leg base. You could make the ends without the bases, so the legs rest directly on the ground, or you could make the legs longer and bury them in the ground for a permanent structure. Two lengthwise rails aid rigidity in that direction.

Decide on the end assembly you want, then make two pairs of legs (FIG. 3-13A). Do not make the notches very deep. Their purpose is mainly for accurate location and ⅜ inch will be deep enough and not affect the strength of each leg.

Cut tenons at top and bottom (FIG. 3-13B and C). They are kept shorter than the thickness of the top and bottom rails because they should not go through and absorb moisture in the end grain.

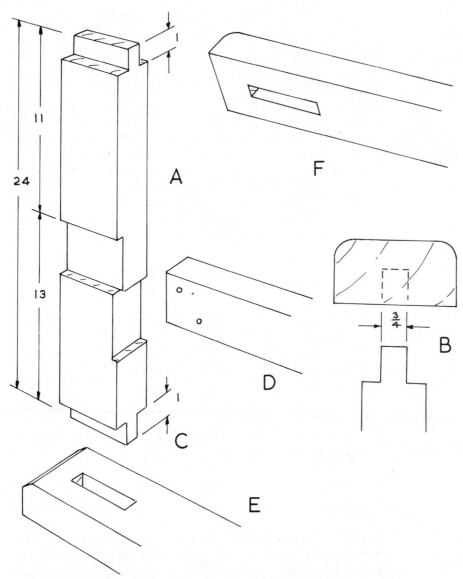

Fig. 3-13. Joints for the ends of the heavy-duty outdoor bench.

Materials List for Heavy Duty Outdoor Bench

7 seat strips	2 × 4 × 74	
spacers from	1 × 3 × 96	
4 legs	2 × 4 × 26	
2 seat rails	2 × 4 × 20	
2 bases	2 × 4 × 22	
2 armrests	2 × 4 × 22	
2 long rails	2 × 4 × 74	

Make the rails to support the seats (FIG. 3-11C and 3-13D). Drill the joints for bolts through both pieces.

Cut the bottom rail (FIG. 3-11D and 3-13E), with mortises for the leg tenons. These rails are shown the same length as the armrests, but if you need a greater spread on soft ground, cut them longer.

Make the armrests in the same way (FIG. 3-11E and 3-13F). Round the top edges and corners.

Take sharpness off edges of all end parts. Bolt the rails in place, then glue the tenons into the other rails. If necessary, drive nails across the tenons.

Join the end assembly to the seat. You can drive nails through the legs into the ends of rails and more nails downwards through the center seat strip.

Prepare the lengthwise rails (FIG. 3-11F) slightly too long. As you nail them in place, check squareness of the seat to each end assembly. Level the rail ends.

If the wood has been treated with colored preservative, it will probably not need any other finish. Otherwise treat it with paint.

ARMCHAIR

An armchair may seem an ambitious project for one weekend, but this chair design (FIG. 3-14) has been arranged so there are many similar parts and operations that can be dealt with together, thereby saving time. The chair could be made in a good furniture hardwood to take its place alongside other furniture indoors. Alternatively, it could be made of softwood or hardwood for use outdoors. In both cases the chair could be used as it is, but comfort would be improved with cushions, preferably made to fit.

The chair is of stout construction so it should stand up to use anywhere, including possible rough handling in a playroom or on a games field. Sizes of wood quoted are recommended, but it does not matter if the wood you obtain is reduced a little by planing. Get all wood planed all around before you start. Several parts are identical. There are a large number of mortise and tenon joints, but nearly all of them are the same, so if you set up your equipment for that size and have all the parts ready for treatment, cutting the joints should not take long. Prefabricate as much as you can before putting any parts together.

The sizes suggested (FIG. 3-15) will produce a chair comfortable for adult use, with or without cushions. The seat is curved and slopes from back to front. The chair back is high enough to provide head support. The arms slope parallel with the seat and are broad enough for writing on.

You need a full-size drawing of the main lines in a side view (FIG. 3-16). Draw this on paper or a spare piece of plywood or hardboard. Draw the front edge of a front leg square to the baseline and draw in its tapered shape (FIG. 3-16A). The resulting sloping rear edge gives you the angles of the seat and back. Draw the seat and arm line square to that line (FIG. 3-16B) and the front surface of the back square to them (FIG. 3-16C). Fill in the other lines shown. Use this drawing to check relevant parts as you make them.

Fig. 3-14. An armchair that may be finished for indoor or outdoor use.

Make the pair of rear legs (FIG. 3-15A and 3-16D). The front edge slopes from a 2 inch width to below the bottom edge of the side seat rail, then tapers back to a 2-inch foot. The rear edge tapers to a width of about 4 inches behind the seat. Blend the two rear slopes into each other with a curve.

Mark on the pair of legs where the seat and lower rails will join the edge and the two back rails will come on the surface. These rails are set back by the thickness of the back slats.

Cut the pair of front legs (FIG. 3-15B and 3-16E), getting the angles of the ends from your full-size drawing. Allow for a ½-inch long tenon at the top ⅝ inch wide.

From your drawing mark where the seat and lower rails come on the edge and the front seat rail on the side.

Plan mortise and tenon joints to suit your equipment. In all the structural joints, the tenons may penetrate 1 inch and be one-third of the thickness of the wood (probably ⅝ inch). In the majority of joints these parts meet squarely (FIG. 3-17A). Have your marking out equipment set to these sizes.

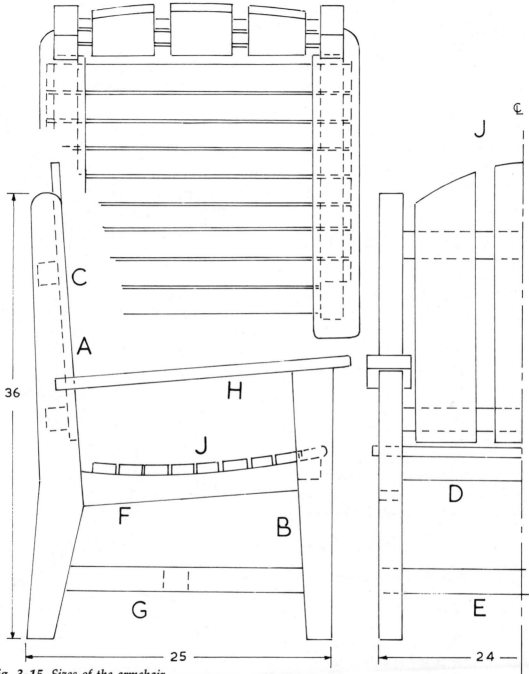

36

C

A

H

J

F

B

G

J

D

E

25

24

Fig. 3-15. Sizes of the armchair.

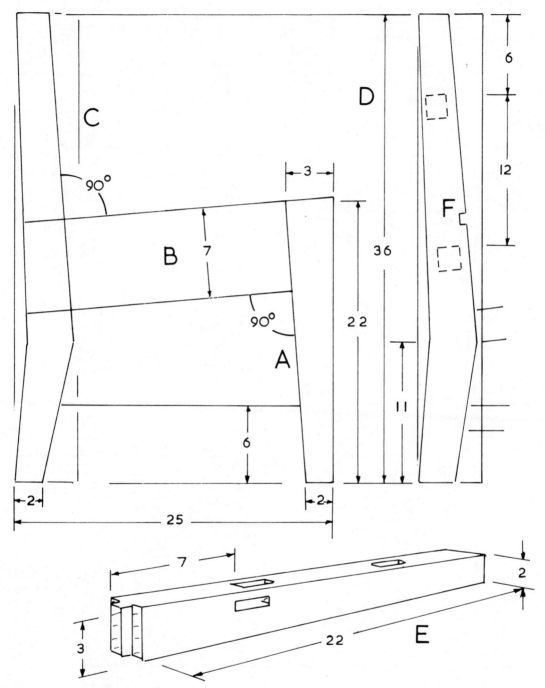

Fig. 3-16. *Proportions and angles of the armchair parts.*

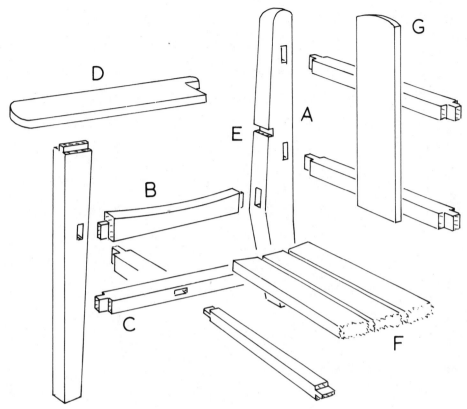

Fig. 3-17. How the armchair parts fit together.

The two back rails (FIG. 3-15C), the front seat rail (FIG. 3-15D) and the lower crossbar (FIG. 3-15E) are all the same (FIG. 3-18A), except the seat rail should be beveled to match the curve of the seat. You can find this angle from the next pieces (FIG. 3-18B).

The side seat rails (FIG. 3-15F, 3-17B and 3-18C) are 2½ inches deep before shaping. Spring a batten to a curve so you can draw the top dipping ½ inch at the center. Cut smoothly to this curve. Reduce the tenons at the ends to 2 inches so they are the same as the other tenons. Check the length with your drawing before cutting.

The lower rails (FIG. 3-15G, 3-17C and 3-18D) have similar tenons to the other rails, but the shoulder will slope to match the legs. Mark the rail length and end angles from your full-size drawing. Mark mortises for the bottom crossbars. This can be central or a little behind the center to give clearance for the sitter's swinging legs.

After marking all tenons, mark their matching mortises and cut the joints.

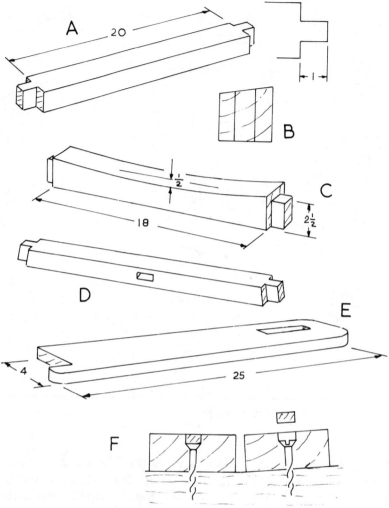

Fig. 3-18. Sizes of parts for the armchair.

Get the sizes for the pair of arms (FIG. 3-15H and 3-17D) from your full-size drawing. Cut notches in the rear legs (FIG. 3-16F and 3-17E) so the arms will fit in ½ inch deep. Let the outside edge of each arm extend a further 1 inch over the rear leg. Allow the front of each arm to extend 2 inches forward of the front legs. Well round the corners and edges.

Mark and cut mortises in the arms to match the tenons on the front legs (FIG. 3-18E and 3-19A). It would be unwise to take the tenons right through because the end grain would be exposed, spoiling appearance and absorbing water if used outdoors. The joint needs to be strong, as the chair may be moved by its arms, so the joint can be strengthened by fox wedging (FIG. 3-19B). Make saw cuts in a tenon and fit short broad-angled wedges, so as the joint is driven together, they are forced in to spread the wood of the tenon.

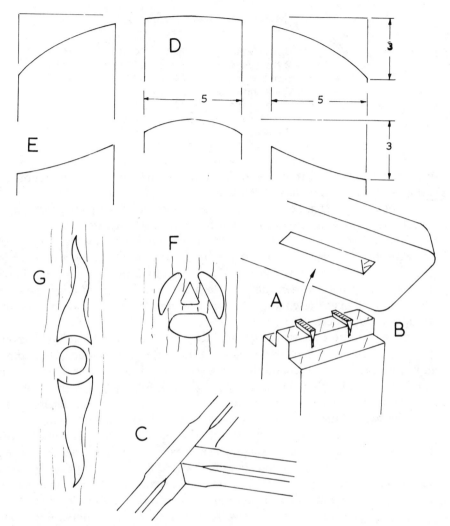

Fig. 3-19. Back and arm details of the armchair.

Check all parts made so far. If the parts are ready, you can assemble the framework without the seat strips and back slats.

Some optional additional work you may wish to do is to lighten the appearance of rails by beveling edges (FIG. 3-19C). This is easily done with a router, or you may use a chisel and small plane. You could do the same on exposed edges of legs and other parts. The effect is to make the wood look smaller.

Assemble the pair of opposite sides first. Join seat and bottom rails to the legs, then add the arms. See that opposite shapes match and the assemblies are without twist. It is advisable to let the glue set in the sides before joining with parts the other way.

The rails across are all the same length, so the chair should assemble squarely if you bring the parts together while the chair is standing on a flat surface. You

Materials List for Armchair

2 rear legs	2 × 5	× 38
2 front legs	2 × 3	× 24
6 rails	2 × 2	× 25
2 seat rails	2 × 2½	× 25
9 seat strips	2 × 2	× 26
3 back slats	¾ × 5	× 25
2 arms	1 × 4	× 26

may have to clear the mortises in the front legs where part of the tenon on the front rail overlaps the ends of the tenons on the seat rail in each leg.

When the glue has set, remove any glue squeezed from joints, and sand parts which may not be as accessible when the other parts are added.

The seat strips (FIG. 3-15J and 3-17F) are shown 2 inches wide. You could use other widths. Cut lengths to overhang by ½ inch at the chair sides. Arrange the strips with ⅛-inch gaps, which will allow water to drain through if used outside. The front strip fits between the front legs and has a rounded edge, extending a short distance over the edge of the rail. The next strip may have to be notched around the front legs.

Glue and screw the seat strips in place. For a painted chair to be used outside you may countersink the screw heads on the surface. For indoor use and a clear finish, it's preferable to counterbore the screw heads and cover them with plugs (FIG. 3-18F). Start fitting the seat strips from the front edge. A piece of ⅛-inch hardboard or plywood may be used as a gauge to regulate the spacing of strips.

The back of the chair is shown with three upright slats (FIG. 3-15J and 3-17G). You could use other numbers and widths. The tops may follow a simple curve (FIG. 3-19D) or you could use other shapings such as the one illustrated (FIG. 3-19E).

Slats may be plain, but you could follow tradition by piercing a pattern in the center one, making an interesting exercise for a scroll saw. Avoid too much detail. You might include an initial (FIG. 3-19F) or use a formal decoration (FIG. 3-19G).

Join the slats to the back rails with glue and screws countersunk or counterbored, as suggested for the seat strips.

Check that the chair stands without rocking on a flat surface. Trim the bottom of one or more legs, if necessary. Bevel around the bottoms of the legs to reduce the risk of splitting or damaging floor covering.

Finish in the chosen way and add fitted cushions if you wish.

CHILD'S CHAIR

A young child likes to have a chair similar to those used by his parents, but it has to be scaled to size and the child does not remain that size for long. Therefore, you might not want to spend a lot of time and skill making an elaborate chair that will only be used for a year or so. Unless, of course, there are other children coming along, or you wish to pass the chair on to another family.

This chair (FIG. 3-20A) should suit a child during his first couple of years. You

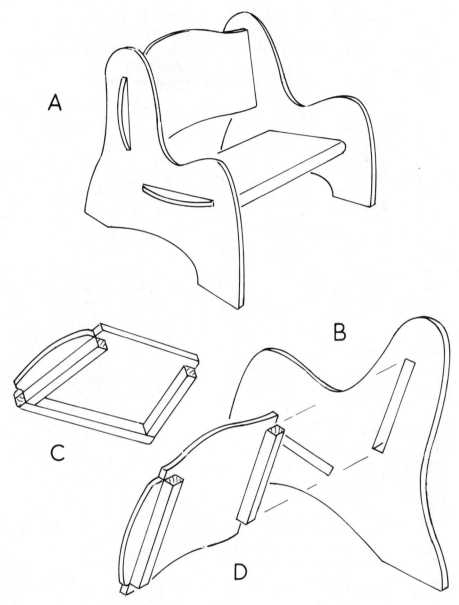

Fig. 3-20. A child's chair made of framed plywood.

could use the same method to make a larger chair by drawing the shapes on larger squares than the 2 inch examples in the drawings. Main parts are ½-inch plywood. If you use softwood plywood be careful of the risk of splintering. Edges should be thoroughly rounded and sanded. Stiffening pieces should have their exposed edges and corners rounded.

If you put the chair together with screws and no glue, you will be able to take it apart without damage, so it can be stored flat when the first user has grown out of it and reassembled later for another child; or you may want to cut it up to make something else. If you expect more than one re-assembly, use hardwood reinforcing pieces as the threads cut in them by the screws are better able to resist stripping then might happen with softwood.

The seat width tapers, but the back is parallel. Tenons go through the sides and you should make these tight fits in their mortises. With the strips screwed inside, the chair should be very rigid and able to endure any child's rough treatment.

Mark out and cut the pair of sides (Fig. 3-20b and 3-21). Check slots against the thickness of the plywood to be used for the seat and back. Round and sand all edges except those that will rest on the floor, but make sure they are not rough.

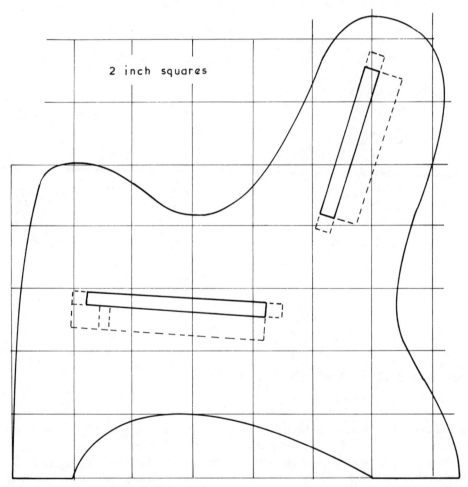

2 inch squares

Fig. 3-21. A side of the child's chair.

The seat (FIG. 3-20C and 3-22A) is tapered. Its tenons go through the sides and project a further ½ inch, which should be rounded in all directions.

Put a stiffening strip under the front edge and round it and the plywood (FIG. 3-22B). Put more strips inside the tenons to come against the sides. Place screws (#6 gauge and 1 inch long) about 3 inches apart through the plywood into the strips for all joints, but make sure the heads are fully countersunk, so there is no risk of scratching small hands.

The back (FIG. 3-20D and 3-22C) has to fit closely between the sides. It should be 8 inches between the tenon shoulders, but you may wish to assemble the seat to the sides and check if there will be slight variations.

Materials List for Child's Chair

2 sides	15 × 15 × ½ plywood
1 seat	27 × 13 × ½ plywood
1 back	8 × 10 × ½ plywood
1 seat front	¾ × ¾ × 12
4 stiffeners	¾ × ¾ × 7

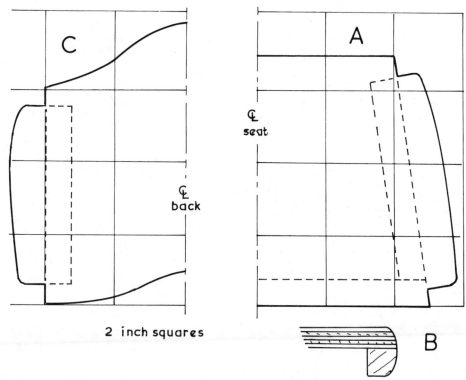

Fig. 3-22. Shapes of the back and seat of the child's chair.

Cut the back to shape and well round the top and bottom edges. The chair will be picked up by gripping under the back. Put strips inside the tenons to come against the sides.

Assemble with screws through the sides. Check that the chair stands on a level surface without rocking. If necessary, plane off one foot.

You might leave the wood untreated if the chair is to be regarded as a play or outdoor item, but it will be advisable to seal the grain against dirt with one or more coats of paint or varnish.

4

Hanging Furniture

Anything hanging on a wall has the advantage of not taking up floor space. If it is shallow back-to-front, the wall provides necessary rigidity and strength. If it is a small item, it can be arranged at the height you want it without needing support from the floor.

Besides the obvious pictures and mirrors, there are shelves and racks that may be wall-mounted. Some furniture that reaches the floor may also need support from a wall to keep it steady. There are also items which have to be hung from the ceiling.

Something to mount on a wall may be the only way to add a useful and attractive item to a room which already appears to be full of furniture. Most pieces of hanging furniture are easy enough to make in a weekend.

HALL MIRROR

As well as a table in the hall, there is a need for a mirror, but because of the usual restricted space, this is best attached to the wall. This simple wall mirror is intended to complement the half-octagonal hall table and hang on the wall above it (FIG. 2-19). It is of matching design, with the angular decoration continued on the shelf.

Sizes are suggested (FIG. 4-2), but you can alter them to suit your needs or an available mirror without affecting the method of construction. Use a hardwood, preferable matching the table or other hall furniture. A mirror is heavy and a simple miter joint at each corner of the frame, as might be satisfactory for a picture, would not be strong enough. Instead, bridle or open mortise and tenon joints are shown (FIG. 4-3A and B).

Fig. 4-1. This framed hall mirror has shelf above and is screwed to the wall.

Prepare sufficient strips for the frame. Cut rabbets and bevel the front edges (FIG. 4-3C). Cut the rabbets to two-thirds the thickness of the wood, so joint widths will be symmetrical.

Mark the overall lengths (FIG. 4-2A), but cut outside the lines so you can plane the projections level after assembly.

Mark the joints. An edge of the tenon and the side of a mortise come level with the inside of the rabbet. Miter the meeting parts at the front (FIG. 4-3D). The frame looks best if the tenons are cut on the horizontal pieces.

Assemble the frame squarely and without twist. Glue alone should be all that is needed in the joints, but if you are doubtful about any of them, drive a screw across the parts from the back where the heads will not normally show.

When the glue has set, plane off projecting ends and remove any excess glue inside.

The shelf (FIG. 4-2B and 4-3E) may be glued and screwed on the top of the frame.

The brackets (FIG. 4-2C and 4-3F) should be exactly square or very slightly more than 90 degrees, so there is no risk of anything on the shelf sliding forward.

There may be a single dowel upwards into the shelf, but you can drive screws from the back of the frame into the upright parts of the brackets.

Do not make the mirror too tight a fit in the frame. There should be about 1/16 inch clearance all around the edges.

Cut a piece of card to cover its back, then make fillets to go around the edges (FIG. 4-3G). Their section will depend on the thickness of the mirror, but they will probably be about 3/8-inch square. Pins should be at about 3-inch intervals.

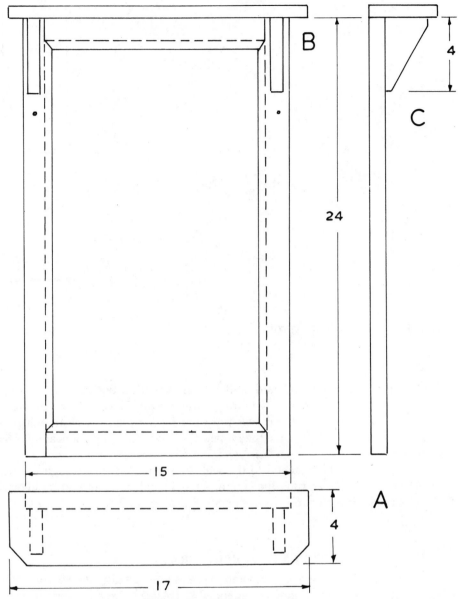

B

C

24

4

15

A

4

17

Fig. 4-2. Suggested sizes for the hall mirror.

Materials List for Hall Mirror

2 frames	$15/16 \times 1 3/4 \times 26$
2 frames	$15/16 \times 1 3/4 \times 17$
1 shelf	$3/4 \times 4 \times 19$
2 brackets	$3/4 \times 2 1/2 \times 6$
2 fillets	$3/8 \times 3/8 \times 24$
2 fillets	$3/8 \times 3/8 \times 15$

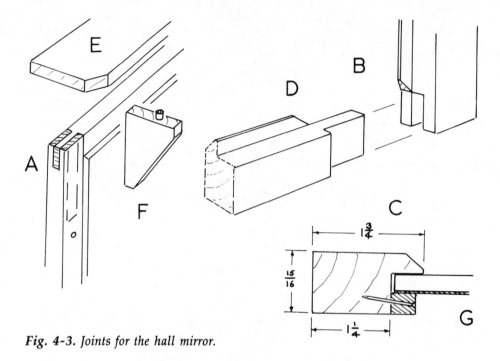

Fig. 4-3. Joints for the hall mirror.

Make sure the mirror, its card, and the fillets will fit, but you may wish to finish the woodwork before finally putting in the mirror. The finish should match the table or other furniture and will probably be stain and a clear polish. A refinement is to paint black inside the rabbet. This gives the mirror a neat reflected border.

The mirror may be attached to the wall by screws driven through an inch below the brackets. Plated roundhead screws would look good, or you could drive flathead screws through cup or countersunk finishing washers.

PLATE DISPLAY RACK

The many available series of decorative plates must be displayed if you are to benefit from the enjoyment they are intended to create. A large number of plates on independent stands will get confusing and risk breakage. It would be better to arrange the plates on narrow shelves on a wall. For the best visual effect the shelves should not be very wide, but there must be no risk of plates falling off. This block of shelves (FIG. 4-4) is not intended to compete with the plates in appearance, but if made of hardwood and given a good finish, it should take its place as a piece of furniture in its own right in any room.

Sizes may have to be adapted to suit the plates you collect. As shown (FIG. 4-5A), there is space for nine 9 inch plates, without crowding them, or you could fit

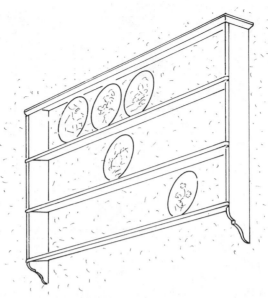

Fig. 4-4. *This display rack is intended to show your plates attractively and safely.*

in more smaller plates. Distances between shelves should be enough for plates to be put in, with a little to spare.

Most construction is with dado joints cut the full width of the ends and with shelves overlapping (FIG. 4-5B). It would be possible to use dowels, but dado joints are preferable.

Mark out the pair of sides (FIG. 4-5C) first. The widths of the grooves should match the actual wood to be used for the shelves. The top will fit into a rabbet the same depth as the grooves (FIG. 4-5D).

Prepare the wood for the three shelves and make the grooves that will retain the plates (FIG. 4-5E). Plow a groove ⅜-inch wide and deep, then bevel its inner edge.

Cut the ends of the shelves to overhang the grooves in the sides (FIG. 4-5F). Round the front edges and the corners.

Make the top (FIG. 4-5G) the same width as the ends and a length to match the shelves.

For screwing the rack to the wall, add a strip to go above the upper shelf (FIG. 4-5H). It may be notched into the ends or merely butt against them. Glue and screw it to the shelf from below.

When all the joints have been cut, shape the lower ends of the sides (FIG. 4-6). Remove any saw marks and round the front edges. Sand all parts before assembly.

Dado joints do not have much strength unaided. The top of the rack may be secured with glue and two or three screws at each end (FIG. 4-5J). Prepare the bottom shelf for two screws to be driven diagonally upwards (FIG. 4-5K) at each end. There should be no need to also do this on the other shelves.

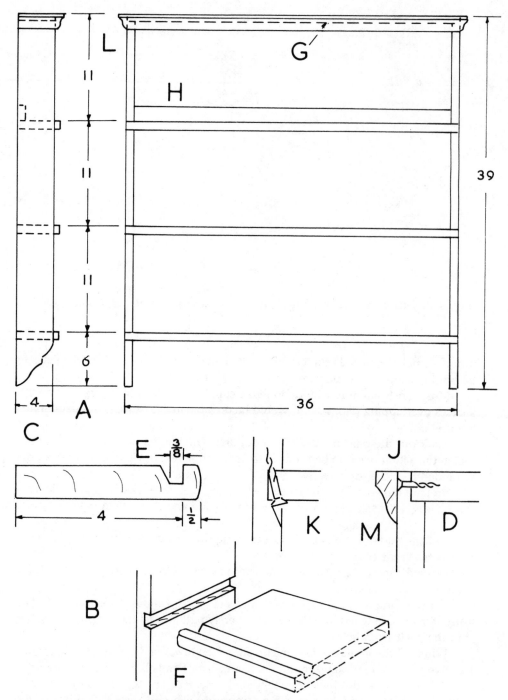

Fig. 4-5. Sizes and details of the plate display rack.

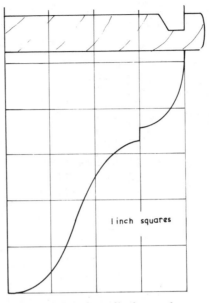

1 inch squares

Fig. 4-6. *The bottom shaping of the plate display rack.*

Materials List for Plate Display Rack

2 ends	$3/4 \times 4 \quad \times 41$
3 shelves	$3/4 \times 4^{1}/_{2} \times 38$
1 top	$3/4 \times 4 \quad \times 38$
1 strip	$3/4 \times 1^{1}/_{2} \times 36$
1 molding	$1/2 \times 1^{1}/_{2} \times 40$
2 moldings	$1/2 \times 1^{1}/_{2} \times 6$

Glue and screw the parts together. Have the rear edges resting on a flat surface to prevent twist. Compare diagonal measurements to check squareness.

At the top use molding about 1½-inch wide, which you can make or buy (FIG. 4-5L and M). Miter the front corners. Attach it with glue and pins sunk below the surface and covered with stopping.

Finish the rack with stain and polish.

BOOK AND DISPLAY SHELVES

Hanging shelves have a large number of uses in many rooms, with the advantage of not taking up possibly restricted floor space. They can take many forms, from purely utilitarian to elaborately decorated, but in most cases they are functional, and much of the decorative value comes from what is put on them. They can be any size or number; this example (FIG. 4-7) is of moderate size, suitable for most books you are likely to possess, and arranged with divisions so you can

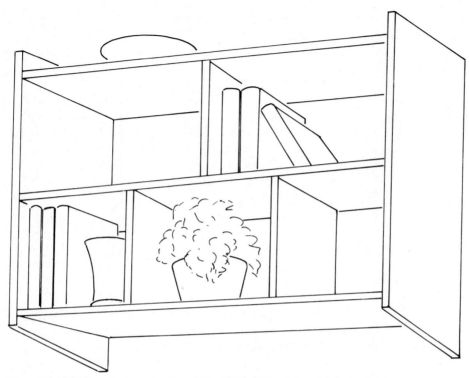

Fig. 4-7. Display shelves on the wall will hold books and many other things.

separate books from display items or keep books upright when a shelf is only partly full. You can easily adapt the design to suit situations and requirements.

The sizes (FIG. 4-8) are based on pieces ¾ inch × 9 inches, with the back strips cut down from one width. You could use solid wood or plywood with solid wood lips on the front edges. The design is particularly suitable for particleboard, bought with its surfaces and edges covered with wood or plastic veneer. Cut ends which are exposed may be covered with iron-on matching veneer strips.

Construction could be with dado joints in solid wood, but these are not so successful in plywood or particleboard, so dowels are suggested throughout. For strength in the shelf to end joints, the dowels are taken right through. If you use a contrasting wood for dowels, the exposed ends may be regarded as decorative features. Dowels 5⁄16 inch or ⅜ inch diameter arranged three in each wide board should be satisfactory.

Make two matching sides (FIG. 4-8A and B). Iron on end strips if you are using veneered particleboard. Mark on the positions of the shelves.

Cut the three shelves (FIG. 4-8C and D), and mark the positions of divisions — the top centrally and the other two dividing the length into three.

Cut the three backs to the same length as the shelves. Two are 3 inches wide (FIG. 4-8E) and the top one 2 inches wide (FIG. 4-8F).

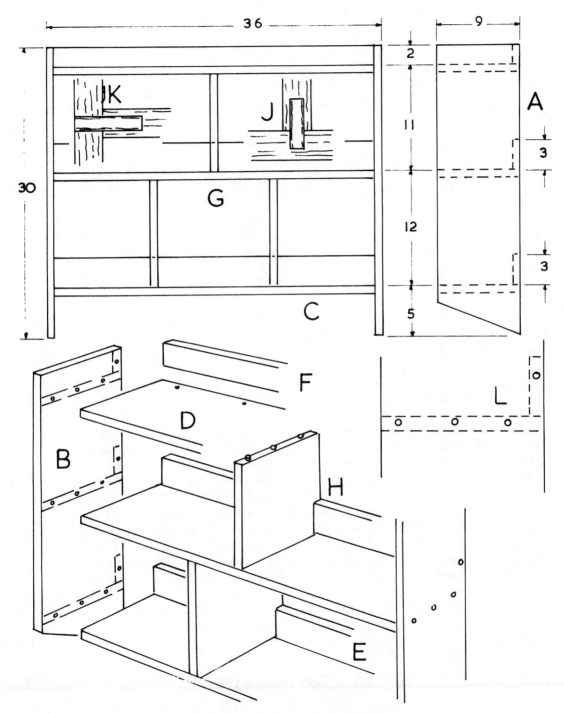

Fig. 4-8. Sizes and assembly details of the book and display shelves.

Materials List for Book and Display Shelves

2 ends	$\frac{3}{4} \times 9 \times 32$
3 shelves	$\frac{3}{4} \times 9 \times 38$
2 divisions	$\frac{3}{4} \times 9 \times 13$
1 division	$\frac{3}{4} \times 9 \times 12$
2 backs	$\frac{3}{4} \times 3 \times 38$
1 back	$\frac{3}{4} \times 2 \times 38$

Attach the backs to their shelves. You could use dowels or screws driven upwards at about 6-inch intervals. Screw heads would not be very obvious in the finished unit.

Make the divisions (FIG. 4-8G), cut away to fit closely over their backs (FIG. 4-8H).

Prepare the divisions and shelves for dowels, which should not go through (FIG. 4-8J).

Join the bottoms of the divisions to their shelves. Screw through the backs into the divisions.

Compare the shelf spacing at division level with your markings on the ends and correct at the ends if necessary. It is important that spacings are the same if the unit is to go together squarely.

Drill the shelves, backs and ends for dowels (FIG. 4-8K and L). Be careful that grain does not break out at the holes on the outside of the ends.

Join the shelves to their divisions and the shelves and backs to the ends. Let dowels project a little, for planing level after the glue has set.

An alternative at the sides, particularly with particleboard, is to screw into the shelves and back, counterboring the screw heads and covering them with plastic plugs, which may be the same or contrasting in color with the main material.

The parts should pull square without difficulty during assembly, but check squareness and see that the parts will lay flat against a wall.

The shelves and a load of books will be quite heavy, so use adequate screws to the wall. A suitable arrangement would be a central screw hole in the top back and one near each end of the other backs. You may then hang the unit at first by the top central screw and level the shelves so you can mark through the other hole positions, then either drill and screw through directly or take the shelves down while you drill and plug the wall.

Finish will depend on the material. Some veneered particleboard may not need any added finish, but wood should be stained and polished to match other furniture.

TALL HANGING CABINET

If the available space is narrow, but there is ample height, you can make a useful cabinet which is considerably higher than it is wide. You might even make it from floor to ceiling, but more likely it will be arranged to hang so the shelves and compartments are within easy reach. There are many ways you can arrange storage, but the example (FIG. 4-9) has some open shelves and one enclosed part which could serve as a medicine cabinet. This has a door that swings down to make a shelf on which you could write or pour medicine.

Most parts are solid wood, which could be hardwood with a finish to match other furniture, but for a bathroom or utility room you might use softwood and paint it. The back is plywood or hardboard, which could extend the full height, but it will be better to use solid wood across at top and bottom, as described below. There are curved decorations shown, but if you prefer a more severe appearance you could simply bevel the ends of the sides. Dado joints are shown for the shelves. Alternatively, you could dowel the shelves in place. To simplify grooving, the shelves are arranged to overhang at the front, so most grooves can be cut right through the skies.

The key parts are the pair of sides (FIG. 4-10A and B). Prepare the wood by cutting rabbets the full length to suit the plywood back. Mark across the positions of all grooves.

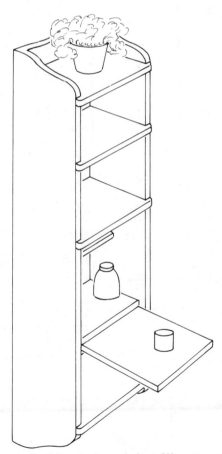

Fig. 4-9. This tall hanging cabinet is intended to fill a narrow space on a wall.

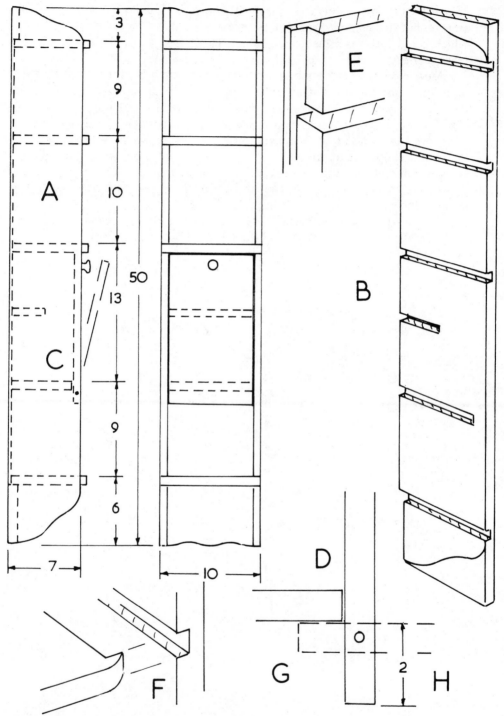

Fig. 4-10. Sizes and details of the tall hanging cabinet.

Cut the grooves to suit the wood that will make the shelves. Stop the groove at the bottom of the cabinet far enough back to allow the door to fit in front of it between the sides (FIG. 4-10C and D). If you want a shelf inside the cabinet, it may be thinner and extend about half the width of the sides.

Widen the rabbets above the top shelf and below the bottom one to take the thicker wood backs (FIG. 4-10E).

Mark the shelves together so all lengths match. Curve the overlapping front corners to finish level with the outsides of the sides (FIG. 4-10F). Final sanding of the curves may be left until after assembly.

Cut the other shelves to fit inside their grooves.

Cut pieces for the solid wood backs to match the shelf lengths.

Draw the curves for the shaped parts (FIG. 4-11). Cut and smooth these edges. Alternatively, leave the backs straight and bevel the ends of the sides.

Making the door can be left until the other parts are assembled, but you should drill for its pivots. These are stout screws (#10 gauge by 2 inches would be

Materials List for Tall Hanging Cabinet

2 sides	$5/8$ ×		7	×	52
4 shelves	$5/8$ ×		7	×	11
1 shelf	$5/8$ ×		$6^1/2$	×	11
1 shelf	$1/2$ ×		3	×	11
1 back	$5/8$ ×		3	×	11
1 back	$5/8$ ×		$5^3/8$	×	11
1 back	10 ×		43	×	$1/4$ plywood

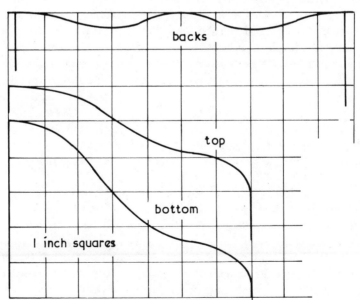

Fig. 4-11. Shaping for the tall hanging cabinet.

suitable), located so the door comes level with the edges when up and rests horizontal when open (Fig. 4-10G).

Glue the shelves into the sides. Clamp tightly, then add the plywood and solid backs. Glue and fine nails will hold the plywood, but use screws through the solid wood. The backs should hold the assembly square, but work on a flat surface so the parts go together without twist.

Cut the door to fit easily between the sides and close to its upper shelf. Allow sufficient overhang at the bottom (Fig. 4-10H) to act as a stop in the open position.

Put the door in position and mark through the screw holes. It may be advisable to use undersize holes first, with loose nails as pivots, to check the action before finally drilling for the screws.

Fit a small knob or handle at the top of the door for pulling it open. A ball catch set in the top of the door will hold it shut.

Drill for screws to the wall. Two screws through the solid wood top will take the weight, and one through the lower back piece will hold it to the wall.

Finish with stain and polish or paint to suit your needs.

HANGING EQUIPMENT RACK

The Shakers had the habit of hanging as much as possible on the wall when the items weren't in use, even including chairs. We may not want to go that far, but besides furniture we attach to the wall or build in, it is worthwhile hanging things when out of use. There are many small things needed about the home, and a container for them can be conveniently hung from a peg or hook. Domestic cleaning items might be kept together this way. Household tools, as distinct from those kept in the shop, might be kept together for lifting down when something needs to be hammered, nails need to be driven, or screws need to be tightened.

This rack (Fig. 4-12) could be used for any of these purposes. The back will go flat against a wall, and the hand hold is shaped so it will hang over a peg or just a nail. There are holes to take tools and a large bin for cloths and other items. Beneath that is a compartment that will take cans of cleaning supplies, boxes of nails and small things that are better enclosed. In front of this is a flap, which acts as a door and can be held up with a turnbutton. When lowered to the floor, it makes a clean surface to lay out what you will be using and to sort out small things safely, if you are working on grass or earth outdoors.

The parts may be plywood and softwood, screwed or nailed together, and finished with paint.

The suggested sizes (Fig. 4-13) should suit most needs, but they could be modified if you want to carry items of other sizes, or the rack has to fit in a particular place. You could make a very similar rack fitted to hold portable power tools and their cables.

Mark out the back plywood panel first, with the positions of the other parts (Fig. 4-13A and 4-14A). The hand and hanging hole is based on three 1-inch diameter holes (Fig. 4-13B), then the top edge is curved around it. Cut the hole and round its edges.

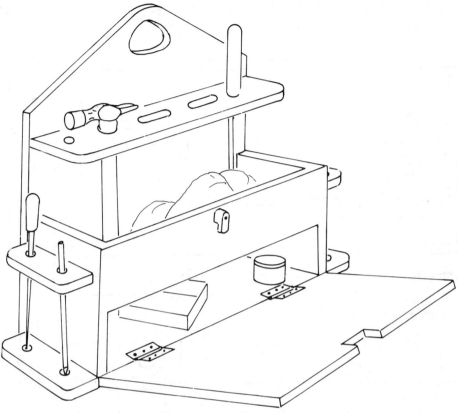

Fig. 4-12. This equipment rack may be used for household or shop tools and may be carried about or hung on a wall.

The pair of solid wood ends (FIG. 4-13C and 4-14B) settle the sizes the other way. Notch the front edges to take the plywood bin front.

Make the bin bottom (FIG. 4-14C) to fit between the ends.

Cut the compartment bottom the same width, but let it extend 3 inches at each end (FIG. 4-13D and 4-14D). Fit strips across the ends to match the extensions (FIG. 4-14E). Drill for tools, with the holes in the bottom only going part way through.

Add a strip with holes to suit your tools high on the back (FIG. 4-13E and 4-14F).

Join the strips to the ends. Screw or nail the bin and compartment bottoms to the ends, then join the back panel to them.

Cut and fit the bin front (FIG. 4-13F and 4-14G).

The flap overlaps the ends and is level with the top of the bin front, but at the bottom it should come level with the upper edge of the compartment bottom, so it can swing down in front of it (FIG. 4-13G and 4-14H).

Position two 2-inch hinges between the bottom and the flap.

Cut a notch in the center of the top edge of the flap (FIG. 4-13H and 4-14H) to clear a turnbutton.

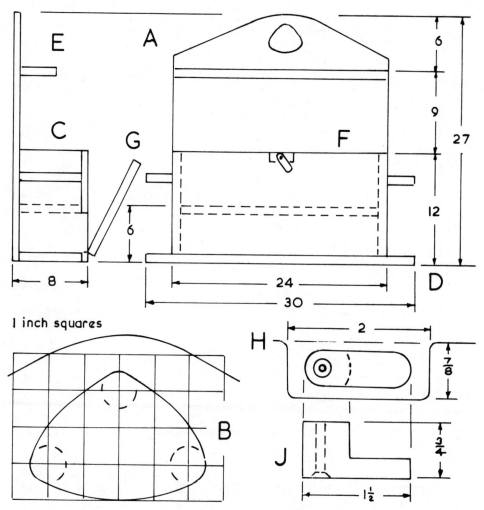

Fig. 4-13. Sizes and details for the hanging equipment rack.

Materials List for Hanging Equipment Rack

1 back	24 × 27 × ½ plywood
1 bin front	6 × 25 × ½ plywood
1 flap	11½ × 25 × ½ plywood
2 ends	⅝ × 7½ × 13
1 bin bottom	⅝ × 7½ × 25
1 compartment bottom	⅝ × 7½ × 31
1 shelf	⅝ × 3 × 25
2 shelves	⅝ × 3 × 8

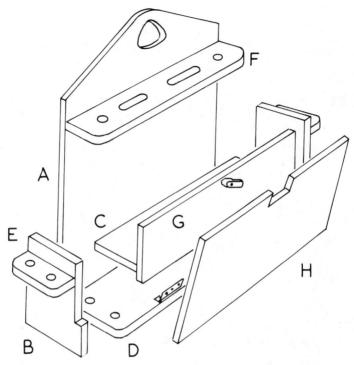

*Fig. **4-14.** How the parts of the hanging equipment rack fit together.*

It is advisable to make the turnbutton of hardwood, even if the rest of the rack is softwood and plywood. Cut it to fit in the flap notch so it will turn over the flap (FIG. 4-13J). You may find it satisfactory to pivot the turnbutton on a woodscrew, but for greater strength use a nut and bolt.

Take sharpness off all exposed edges and corners, then finish with paint. A light color inside will make the contents easier to see.

HANGING TOOL CABINET

In many workshops the most convenient place for the majority of tools is on the wall, preferably within reach of your bench. There is a limit to what can be hung on pegboard or racks and shelves attached directly to the wall, and there is the added problem that tools less often used get dusty and dirty. If there are edge-cutting tools such as chisels, there is a risk that you may dull the edges or cut yourself if they are not protected.

If you make a tool cabinet or cupboard with a door, the tools will be enclosed when not required. This hanging tool cabinet (FIG. 4-15) provides main storage space covered by a pair of doors which also my have racks and fittings for many other tools; then when open, the doors swing back against the wall or fit into a corner (FIG. 4-16), so you have all your equipment exposed where you have it within reach. When you have finished work, the cabinet can be closed, so its contents are protected as well as hidden from prying hands. If the situation

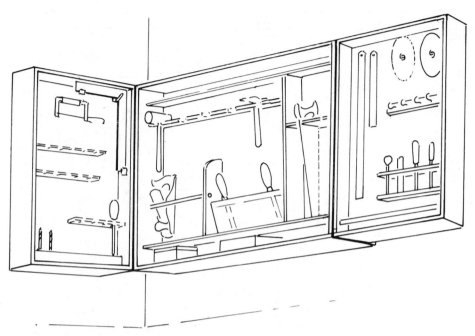

Fig. 4-15. This hanging tool cabinet has racks in the doors and can be closed to secure the tools.

demands it, you could fit a lock. You might make a simple cabinet entirely in one weekend, but if you want to fit in a large number of tools, it may be better to make the main parts in the first weekend, then spend a second weekend fitting them out.

An accumulation of tools can be quite heavy, particularly when concentrated on the hanging screws through the back of a cabinet, so make sure there are suitable strong points on the wall. You may have to alter the position and size of the cabinet. The suggested sizes (FIG. 4-16) are 36 inches square with the main part projecting 6 inches from the wall and the doors a further 4 inches. Check if this will be convenient over your bench area. Measure the depth needed for the tools you want to accommodate. Do not make the tolerances too tight. You may not always have the same tools and should allow for possible changes. Shallower doors will hold flatter things like rules, squares, and some saws, but the suggested sizes will hold thicker tools like gauges, small planes, and light power tools. You will probably have no difficulty in filling the main cabinet, so check the sizes of tools that will then have to go in the doors.

You could make the cabinet of solid wood with plywood panels, but ¾ inch plywood is suggested throughout. This is strong and will not shrink or warp and is thick enough for screws. It should take the heavy loads if properly jointed and secured.

You have to construct three boxes so the two that form the door will fit in front of the main part. It will probably be best to make the main part and use that as a guide to the sizes and squareness of the two front boxes as you make them. If

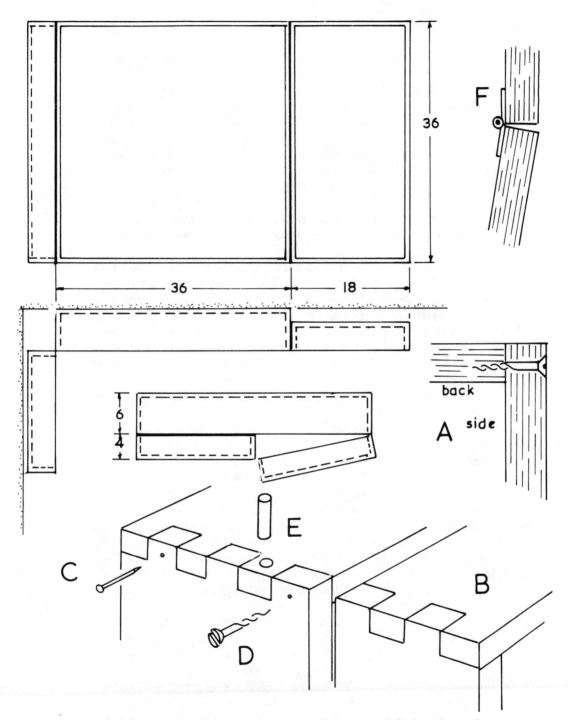

Fig. 4-16. Suggested sizes and construction of parts of the carcass of the hanging tool cabinet.

the main box is not perfectly square, that may not matter if you make the door boxes to match.

For strength and neatness it is advisable to fit the backs and fronts inside the other parts (FIG. 4-16A), with glue and screws at about 3 inch intervals.

There are several possible ways of joining the corners, but plywood does not join satisfactorily with some of the joints suitable for solid wood. You could merely overlap the pieces and use screws, but there is a risk of movement or opening under load. A safe and easy joint for plywood is the finger joint, with interlocking fingers about 1 inch wide (FIG. 4-16B). Glue does not hold well to the end grain of plywood, but in this joint the glue can be reinforced by fastenings both ways, so the pieces cannot be pulled apart without breaking.

Nails are simple and satisfactory fastenings (FIG. 4-16C) through every finger, but if nails seem too crude for your idea of craftsmanship, you can use screws (FIG. 4-16D). If you would rather not have metal fastenings, you could use ¼-inch dowels in every finger (FIG. 4-16E).

Make the main box completely, with its back enclosed and the outsides of the finger joints leveled. Make the sides of the front boxes to match the rear box sides, then the tops and bottoms to allow a small clearance at the center. For most purposes the meeting of the front boxes should be at the center, but if it would suit your situation better, as when opening to a limited space in a corner or when a particularly wide tool has to fit in one door, one box could be wider than the other. Complete the front boxes and check their fit. Outer corners of all boxes and front edges of the doors may be rounded.

The best hinges are the continuous 'piano' type, going the full length of the sides. The alternative is to swing the doors on three 3 inch hinges each side. Plywood does not take hinge screws satisfactorily on edge, so the hinges should be on the outside (FIG. 4-16F).

Fit the hinges with a few screws for a trial assembly, but you may need to separate the parts while making the internal fittings. It is advisable at this stage to decide where the cabinet is going on the wall and where you will put the screws to fasten it there. It is the screws near the top which have to take most of the downward load and prevent the cabinet tipping forward. Have at least two long thick screws into strong points in the wall as near the top as you can reasonably arrange them, then others a little further down and two near the bottom to keep the back close to the wall. Mark inside the back where these screw holes should come. You may have to modify the positions (if wall conditions will allow) when you lay out fittings to take tools.

Assemble the tools you hope to put in the cabinet. Have the cabinet parts flat on the bench and try various arrangements. You will probably want to include boxes of small items, so allow shelves for them. Some tools will go in edgewise, while others will have to be flat. Some tools will fit in front of others. For instance, drills could fit into holes on a shelf that also has tools fitted into slots, while others may hang on hooks in front. However, do not crowd tools too much. It will be a nuisance if you have to remove one tool to get at another. An exception might be a little-used tool that could go behind one you are always reaching for. Shallower and lighter tools may go in the doors, and there may be squares and other tools large one way and shallow the other that would be best in a door.

If you screw in the fittings you make to hold tools and do not use glue, you can change your mind later or alter the layout to suit different tools. So far as possible arrange tools to be taken out by pulling forward, rather than by lifting. A short lift may be acceptable; but if you put a row of screwdrivers through holes and they have to be lifted 5 inches to take out, there may not be enough clearance above to do that, or the space above may not be available to accommodate another tool.

As a woodworker you will want to make most of the fittings of wood, but do not neglect some metal and plastic helps that are available. A row of spring clips on a batten or edge of a shelf (FIG. 4-17A) will hold many handled tools, but do not use them for very heavy items. If a tool will hang on a nail, there may be no need for anything more elaborate. You could cut off the head of the nail and tilt it upwards (FIG. 4-17B), or you could screw in a cup hook, possibly with its end cut to a shorter bend (FIG. 4-17C). It might be possible to include a piece of pegboard to take some of the ready-made hooks designed to fit it, but for tools inside the swinging doors it is better to have something more positive so they are held flat.

You will have to lay out the parts of the cabinet to suit your requirements, but the notes that follow suggest how tools can be held. You can combine some of them, so more than one tool can be held on a fitting made from one piece of wood. You may arrange a strip of wood right across and have different types of holding arrangements as needed. Some holding arrangements depend on thin or short-grained parts of the wood, so choose strong close-grained hardwood for racks, as far as possible. If this is given a varnished finish and any exposed screw heads are brass or plated, the interior of the cabinet will look smart and thereby encourage you to do good work with the tools.

You could make boxes to contain small items, but it will be better to get metal or plastic containers which can be labeled and put on shelves. If the top of the cabinet will be fairly high, you might put a shelf for rarely-needed small items there. Otherwise, there could be a row of boxes for screws, nails and other small items on the bottom of the main compartment, possibly with a shelf above (FIG. 7-17D). There will always be a few things you want to put in the cabinet between jobs and for which there is no rack: the shelf is the place. Screw a shelf to cleats on the ends of the cabinet (FIG. 4-17E).

Shorter round items such as drills and router bits may fit into holes in thick wood. Drill to a regular depth, at least ¾ inch (FIG. 4-17F). There should be no difficulty with clearance above when lifting this short distance.

For longer round tools, they must be put in or out of racks by a forward movement. Allow the lower ends to rest loosely in holes drilled partly through a shelf, but cut notches in a top shelf, then hold the tools in with turnbuttons. There may have to be an individual turnbutton, but on a row of slots you can let a turnbutton cover two slots (FIG. 4-17G). Pivot each turnbutton on a roundhead screw with a washer under the head. You can use this type of rack for tools with wide ends. Screwdriver tips may go into round holes, but a tool with a wide end,

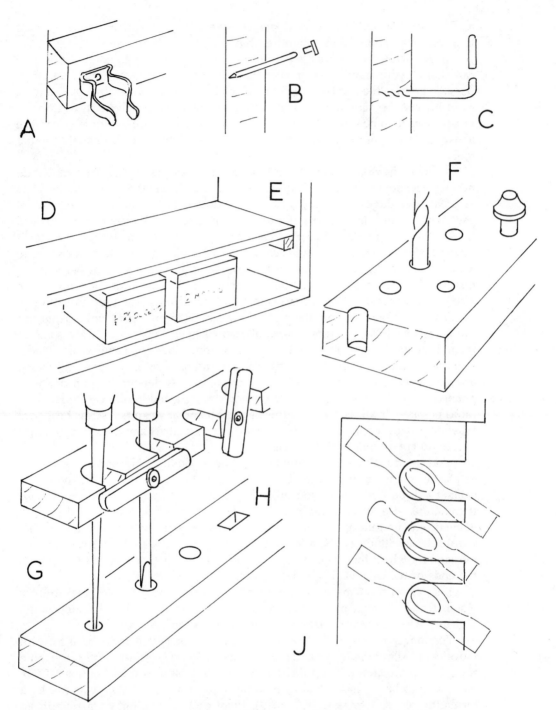

Fig. 4-17. Some methods of fitting out the interior of the hanging tool cabinet.

such as a chisel, could have a shaped socket (FIG. 4-17H). Do not make any of these fittings a close fit on the tools — you need to be able to move them in or out easily. Some tools do not need the lower support. Marking gauges and other tools with long stems or handles only need a notch closed with a turnbutton. Heavier tools such as hammers can have their own rather stronger notched strips. You can economize on space by positioning hammer heads diagonally (FIG. 4-17J).

If there is enough depth front to back, handsaws and some other tools might go into slots without turnbuttons. You could use ½ inch plywood with brackets underneath (FIG. 4-18A). A try square might go into a similar slot or it may need one the other way (FIG. 4-18B). This is a situation where you could include slots, hooks or clips for other tools along the front edge. One way of holding a square is on a block with a lip (FIG. 4-18C). The end of the blade could be held by another block. You may be able to arrange squares of different sizes in front of each other. Another way of dealing with a large square in the corner of a door is to rest on blocks, with a turnbutton at the corner (FIG. 4-18D). Similar methods can be used for many other tools.

Saws need their teeth protected. This can be done by arranging them against the edges of doors. The tip may go in a slotted block (FIG. 4-18E) and the handle held by a shaped block and turnbutton (FIG. 4-18F). You may find satisfaction making the block to be a reasonably shaped fit inside the handle, but a simple parallel block will hold just as well.

A problem with planes is their depth. You may have to store them on shelves, but if there is enough cabinet depth front to back they can fit over a rail (FIG. 4-19A). Even if the depth of a plane is more than the depth of the main compartment, you may be able to allow clearance inside the door. The rail could be supported by one side of the cabinet, and the other end could be on part of another rack. Much depends on the number and sizes of your planes, as well as clearance for lifting them out.

Chisels and gouges may be kept in racks similar to those already described; because of their sharp ends they need special attention, yet you want to be able to identify them easily. You can protect the tools with Plexiglass or other clear plastic, so you can see the blades. Several chisels may go through one long slot made by putting a strip of wood with spacers in front of a shelf edge. If that is sloped, you can pull the tool out without interfering with anything above (FIG. 4-19B).

If you have several portable power tools you may be able to fit them through holes in shelves. It may be better to have stowage for them elsewhere. An electric drill or power tool of similar size may take up an inordinate amount of space with its cable, occupying parts of a cabinet where you could more usefully store hand tools. Most power tools, whether portable or not, have several accessories or parts to be fitted for particular purposes. You may find it worthwhile making racks for these parts in one door, together with wrenches, keys and other special equipment needed for power tools, and sometimes mislaid.

Your cabinet will probably be mounted on the wall with a gap between it and the bench top. You may be able to use its underside. There could be brackets

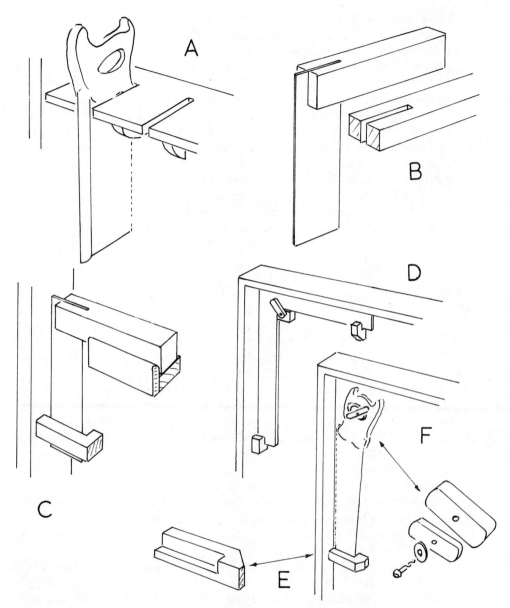

Fig. 4-18. Racks for squares and saws in the hanging tool cabinet.

underneath the ends to provide extra support and end attachments for one or more rails to hang more tools on. There could be hooks underneath for bench brush, push sticks, cables, templates and other items.

Finish your cabinet with paint. Bare wood may seem compatible with shop conditions, but it gets dirty. Bright colors inside and outside are cheerful and make finding tools easier. Varnish on hardwood parts has a workmanlike appearance.

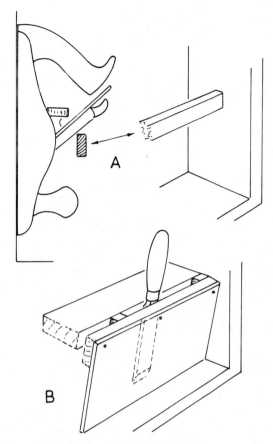

Fig. 4-19. Plane and chisel racks in the hanging tool cabinet.

You may leave your cabinet without door fasteners, but the doors may tend to swing open. In the usual position on the wall, catches underneath are convenient. Any type or clip fastener can be used between the doors and the underside of the main part. If you want to lock the cabinet, put a bolt inside one door to engage with a hole in the bottom of the main part, then fit a lock inside the other door to engage with a slot in the first door and a keyhole to the front. Another way is to put a hasp and staple across the fronts of the doors and use a padlock.

5

Stands and Racks

Some usually smaller and simpler pieces of furniture of use in many rooms are stands and racks of various sorts. They can be fitted in among major items in places unsuitable for another large piece. They will hold things like books, magazines, flowers, and ornaments in a living room, or towels and blankets in a bedroom or bathroom. Outside they can hold pot plants or floral displays.

Many of these stands and racks can be made with smaller pieces of wood, some of which may be offcuts from larger work, so they are economical. With wood that is easy to handle, you do not need large shop space or elaborate equipment. The projects described in this chapter are free standing, so they could be moved about. Some projects with comparable functions, which attach to a wall, are described in Chapter 4.

With a comparatively small project you may use any available wood. If it contrasts with the wood finish of the general furniture in the room, that may be visually pleasing, which it might not be if larger. You might even put a painted stand among polished hardwood furniture.

PLANT STAND

A plant in a pot is best displayed above the floor. It may go on a table or shelf, but if it is to be alone, it needs a stand which is stable against accidental knocks. Although the stand should be presentable, its main visual requirement is to emphasize the beauty of the plant. This plant stand (FIG. 5-1A) is of simple and substantial construction. If made of softwood and painted, it would be suitable for use on a patio or deck. It could be taken indoors, but for more permanent indoor use it would be better made of a hardwood with a polished finish.

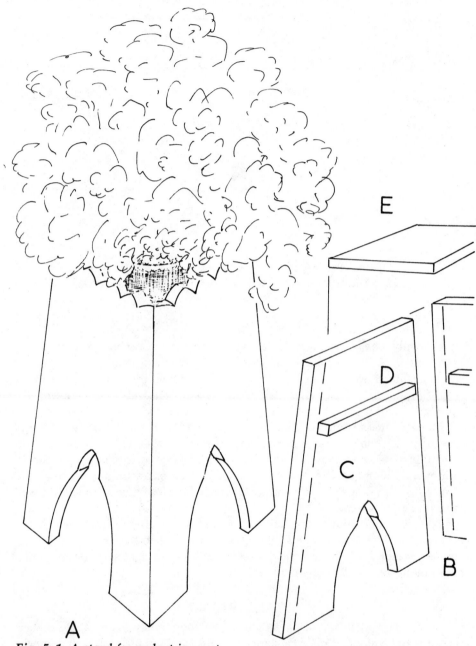

Fig. 5-1. A stand for a plant in a pot.

The sizes suggested (FIG. 5-2) will take a pot up to 9 inches diameter. It is shown with the pot supported 5 inches below the rim of the stand, but you can arrange the shelf height and other dimensions to suit a particular plant and pot. The height of 18 inches is intended to suit a plant with high and spreading foliage.

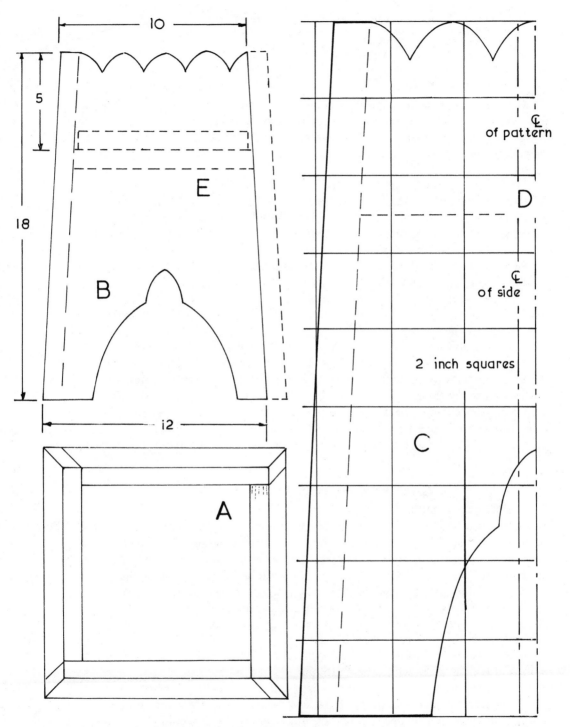

Fig. 5-2. Sizes and the side shapes for the plant stand.

Materials List for Plant Stand

4 sides	1 × 12 × 20
4 cleats	1 × 1 × 10
1 shelf	1 × 9 × 9

The main construction is with four identical sides that have staggered joints, so each board overlaps the next (FIG. 5-1B) in turn around the square (FIG. 5-2A). This means that when you mark out the patterns, they have to be symmetrical on the assembled side and not symmetrical on the piece of wood, as will be explained in the instructions.

Make four sides (FIG. 5-1C and 5-2B), cutting first to the outlines.

Use the squared drawing (FIG. 5-2C) to mark out the patterns. To allow for the extra thickness of the overlapping piece at one side only, draw the patterns about a centerline $\frac{1}{2}$ inch from the centerline of the wood (FIG. 5-2D). Cut the patterns and remove saw marks from the edges.

Fit cleats to support the shelf (FIG. 5-1D and 5-2E) at a height to suit the pot. Use waterproof glue and a few nails or screws.

Glue and screw the sides to each other in turn. If you want to fit the shelf closely all around, include it as you assemble the sides. The alternative is to make it small enough to drop in the top opening and leave it loose on the cleats, so you can remove it occasionally for cleaning (FIG. 5-1E). If the stand is to be used outdoors you might drill a few drainage holes in the shelf, but for indoor use it may be better to fit it closely with waterproof glue so any water that drains from the pot cannot run through to the floor.

Round the outer corners and take sharpness off all exposed edges. Most woods for outdoor use should be treated with preservative, which might be followed with paint. For indoor use you may prefer to finish a hardwood with stain and polish.

GARDENER'S DISPLAY STAND

Display stands can have many uses, but this one is particularly intended for the enthusiastic gardener (FIG. 5-3), although many other uses are obvious. A gardener may use this stand in a greenhouse or other building. The broad area serves as a work surface, the shelves may carry boxes or plant pots or seed trays. The cupboard has ample space for a reserve stock of boxes and other items a gardener accumulates. In the winter the stand could be wheeled indoors and used to display pot plants or carry seedlings or other gardening preparations for the next outdoor growing season. With casters underneath, the stand can be moved for convenience or the benefits of window light.

Most makers will use softwood and finish the stand with paint, but if the stand is to take its place with other furniture indoors, it could be made of hardwood and given a clear finish. The sizes suggested (FIG. 5-4) allow for two shelves and a cupboard with a lift-out door. This allows maximum access to the interior. It would be possible to have one or a pair of hinged doors if that would be preferable. The shelves are open at the back, which will give scope for foliage to hang and

Fig. 5-3. This gardener's display stand can be moved for use indoors or outdoors.

get the best light, but you could continue the plywood back of the cupboard upwards if you want closed shelving for other purposes.

The main sizes are based on 9-inch boards joined to make up the 18 inch width. Slight variations in width will not matter and you should start by joining boards for the ends (FIG. 5-4A and 5-5A). At the same time, join boards to make up widths for the counter and bottom.

Mark the positions of other parts on the ends. The dado grooves should match the actual wood being fitted into them. The counter fits into a groove in the rear board, but rests on the top of the front board (FIG. 5-5B).

Cut the bottom (FIG. 5-5C) to fit between the sides. Prepare its ends and the sides for dowels (FIG. 5-5D), which may be ⅜ inch at about 3-inch spacing.

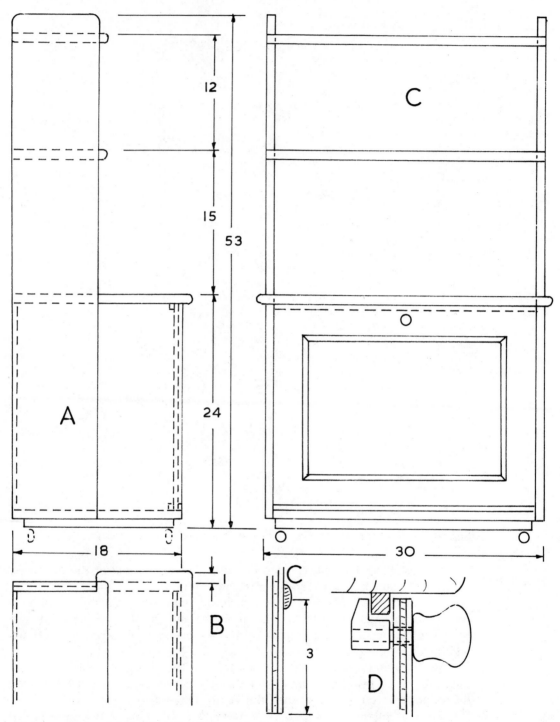

Fig. 5-4. Sizes of the gardener's display stand.

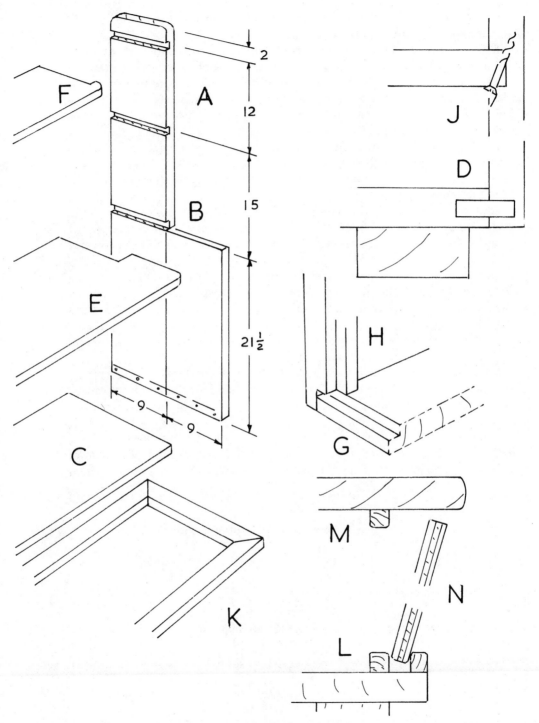

Fig. 5-5. Constructional details of the gardener's display stand.

Cut the counter to fit in the grooves and extend 1 inch at the sides and front (FIG. 5-4B and 5-5E) with rounded edges and corners.

Make the two shelves (FIG. 5-4C) to extend forward 1 inch. Notch them round the sides (FIG. 5-5F) to cover the grooves. Round the front edges and corners.

The plywood back of the cupboard has to be set in level. Cut rabbets on the underside of the counter and the top of the cupboard bottom (FIG. 5-5G). With a suitable router cutter, you could cut rabbets in the sides between these positions, but the alternative is to put strips inside (FIG. 5-5H).

Join the two sides with all the horizontal parts. Glue alone may be sufficient, but you can strengthen with one or more screws driven upwards in the top shelf joints (FIG. 5-5J). You may also need to drive pocket screws upwards under the front part of the counter.

Glue and screw or nail the back plywood behind the cupboard. This should hold the assembly square, but check by comparing diagonal measurements.

Make the base (FIG. 5-5K) keeping it 1 inch from the front and sides, but level at the back. Glue and screw it on.

Use ½-inch square strips to hold the lift-out door. At the bottom, put one piece across level with the front edge. Put another across, leaving a gap that will allow the door to drop in easily (FIG. 5-5L). Round the top edges. Fix with glue and pins.

Put a similar strip across under the counter directly above the inner bottom strip (FIG. 5-5M). This acts as a door stop.

Make the plywood door with a little clearance at the sides and enough clearance at the top to fit in easily (FIG. 5-5N). The plainness of the front can be broken by gluing and pinning on half-round molding (FIG. 5-4C) to form a framed panel.

The fastener for the door is a knob connected to a turnbutton that closes over the door stop inside (FIG. 5-4D). If you turn your own, make the knob with a dowel long enough to go through. If you buy a knob, glue a ⅜ inch dowel centrally in it.

Materials List for Gardener's Display Stand

2 sides	$\frac{7}{8} \times 9 \times 55$
2 sides	$\frac{7}{8} \times 9 \times 25$
2 bottoms	$\frac{7}{8} \times 9 \times 30$
2 counters	$\frac{7}{8} \times 10 \times 34$
2 shelves	$\frac{7}{8} \times 10 \times 32$
1 back	$23 \times 30 \times \frac{1}{2}$ plywood
2 bases	$1 \times 2 \times 30$
2 bases	$1 \times 2 \times 18$
3 door guides	$\frac{1}{2} \times \frac{1}{2} \times 30$
1 door	$23 \times 30 \times \frac{1}{2}$ plywood
2 door moldings	$24 \times \frac{1}{2}$ half-round
2 door moldings	$17 \times \frac{1}{2}$ half-round

Make the turnbutton with a hole to glue on the dowel and a projecting end to turn behind the stop.

Small casters will probably attach to the corners of the base, but if you use larger industrial casters you may have to put blocks inside the base. In any case, keep the casters as close as possible to the corners for stability.

There are no shelves shown in the cupboard, since a gardener may store things of varied sizes at different times; but you could put cleats on the sides for a removable shelf to rest on.

Remove any excess glue and sand where necessary, then finish the stand with several coats of paint, preferably a good exterior type because it is likely to get wet.

ONE-BY-TWO BOOKCASE

Most bookcases have horizontal shelves, which is fine when you want to find a book at near eye level, but a nuisance when the book you're looking for is just above floor level and you have to get on your knees to find it. It would be better if the shelves were tilted, so the titles on the backs of the books could be seen without bending. This bookcase (FIG. 5-6) has two tilted book troughs and a flat shelf above them.

The total height is 33 inches, but the design is arranged so you can make two similar bookcases and fit one on top of the other, giving an assembly which puts the highest shelf at above eye level. The two bookcases may always be separated and used independently if that would better suit a new room layout.

Nearly all of the construction is with 1- × 2-inch strips, which could be hardwood or softwood, doweled together. There are some dowel rod rails and the shelves have panels which could be 1/8 inch hardboard or 1/4 inch plywood.

Although the book troughs are the same, they are arranged so books up to 8 inches by 11 inches may be put on the lower shelf, and books up to 9 inches high on the upper book shelf, to clear below the flat top shelf. You may wish to check the sizes of your books before laying out your own bookcase. The length suggested is 30 inches and the overall height is 33 inches (FIG. 5-7). The shelf length may be varied to suit your needs or available space. Trough angles are 15°.

There are seven frames to be made. Use two 3/8-inch dowels in each corner joint. You might use 1/2-inch dowels, but they would have to be rather close where there are rabbets or cutouts.

Make the two end frames (FIG. 5-7A). Mark the location of the troughs and shelf. Arrange two pairs of 1/2-inch dowel rods across at the open ends of the trough (FIG. 5-7B).

There are notches at the top corners (FIG. 5-7C) and matching cutouts at the bottom (FIG. 5-7D). These serve as decoration and feet, but they also allow one bookcase to be fitted on top of the other if you make a pair. If that is your intention, put a short dowel under each bottom rail (FIG. 5-7E) and a matching hole in the top of what will be the lower bookcase. These are to prevent sideways movement of the assembly. If you do not intend fitting two bookcases together

Fig. 5-6. This bookcase is made mostly of strips and dowel rods.

and are only making one, you may prefer to shape the bottom notch between feet and round the top of the frame.

Make the two trough back frames the same (FIG. 5-7F and 5-8A). Let the upright rails overlap the horizontal ones. Include ½ inch dowel rods across the centers.

Make the two trough shelves (FIG. 5-7G and 5-8B) in a similar way, but arrange the long rails to overlap the short ones. Rabbet the upper edges to take the hardboard or plywood panels. At the corners, cut back the rabbets for the joints (FIG. 5-8C). It is important that these and the previous frames are exactly the same length.

Make the top shelf (FIG. 5-7H and 5-8D) in the same way as the trough shelves, but to the same width as the two upright end frames. It should be sufficient to only use glue in the panels in these frames, but you could drive a few pins, if necessary.

Join the trough backs to their shelves. You may use dowels at about 6-inch intervals, but if the bookcases will be standing against a wall, you could use screws at the same spacings since their heads will not show.

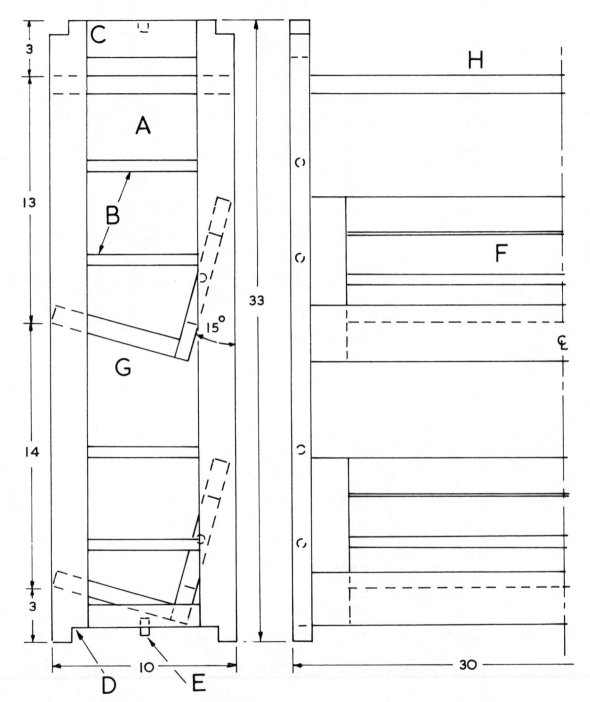

Fig. 5-7. Sizes of the one-by-two bookcase.

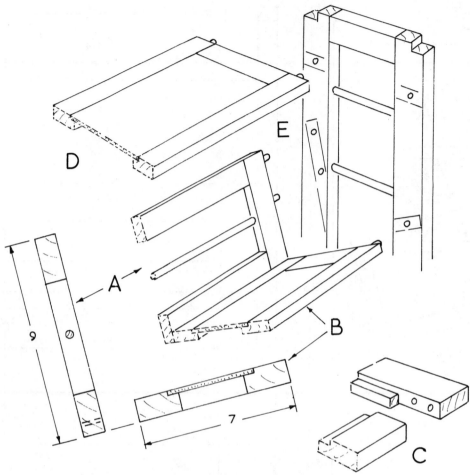

Fig. 5-8. Assembly of parts of the one-by-two bookcase.

Materials List for One-by-Two Bookcase

4 uprights	$1 \times 2 \times 35$
10 rails	$1 \times 2 \times 30$
14 rails	$1 \times 2 \times 11$
2 rails	$30 \times \frac{1}{2}$ diameter
8 rails	$10 \times \frac{1}{2}$ diameter
2 panels	$5 \times 28 \times \frac{1}{8}$ hardboard or $\frac{1}{4}$ plywood
1 panel	$8 \times 28 \times \frac{1}{8}$ hardboard or $\frac{1}{2}$ plywood

Try the troughs in position on the end frames, and correct your previous markings if there are differences, but make sure opposite ends match so that the bookcase assembles squarely.

Drill for two ½-inch dowels where each trough back crosses an upright, but at other crossings there will be single dowels (FIG. 5-8E).

Take sharpness off all edges and sand surfaces before assembly.

Assemble the crosswise parts tightly to one end frame first, then dowel to the other end frame. The parts should pull each other square, but check accuracy by doing the final assembly on a flat surface.

Finish with stain and polish or with paint, as you prefer. The shelf and troughs might be given a finish in contrast to the ends.

TOWEL OR BLANKET RACK

A set of rails on which things can be hung has uses in many parts of the house. In a bathroom, a rack with rails can be used for towels. In a bedroom, the rack may support sheets, blankets or other bed coverings when not needed. In a laundry room, wet clothing may be spread to dry or air. This rack (FIG. 5-9) has three top rails and a middle one for hanging, then two low rails that provide stiffness and also serve as shoe racks. Two top rails extend to crossbars which serve as handles or places to put belts or ties.

The rack is shown 36 inches long and high, with a width of 12 inches, but you could alter any of these sizes to suit your needs or available space. The rails are 1-inch dowel rods and the available lengths may determine length of the rack. As drawn (FIG. 5-10) the proportions should produce a stable piece of furniture. If you alter sizes, be careful not to make the ends so narrow that there is a risk of tipping.

The ends are best made of solid wood, which may be chosen to match other furniture. Alternatively, you could use ¾-inch plywood and give the rack a painted finish. In any case the dowel rods for the rails should be hardwood. If joints are a good fit, glue alone should produce a rigid rack, but choose a water-resistant type for bath or laundry room use.

It is important that holes are drilled squarely in the ends, so the assembly stands upright and without twist. Use a drill press, if possible, or have a guide that holds your hand drill true. Alternatively, have a helper sight your drill if you work freehand. For those holes that do not go right through, drill as deep as possible for maximum strength.

Mark out and cut the pair of ends together. Locate all hole positions first (FIG. 5-11), then draw and cut the outlines. Drill through for the rails that will take the handles, and make the other holes as deep as possible without the drill point breaking through. Use a Forstner bit, if you have one, to get the greatest depth. Use a stop on the drill to get all blind holes the same depth.

Smooth and round all outer edges. The ends are the most prominent parts and will benefit in appearance from good sanding.

Make the two handles (FIG. 5-10A and B). Get the spacing for the handle holes by marking through the holes in the ends. Round the edges and ends thoroughly. You could thin the center part of each handle, if you wish.

Cut the four rails that will go into the blind holes the same length and the

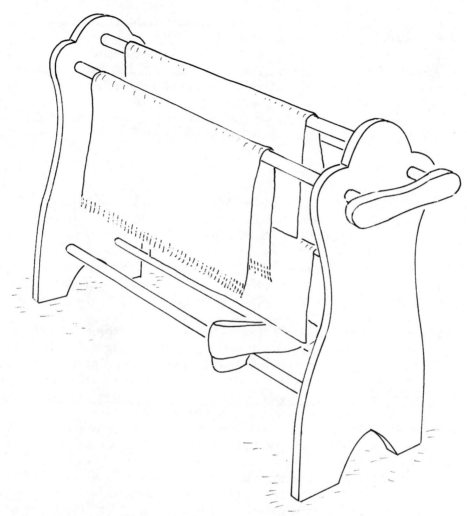

Fig. 5-9. This towel or blanket rack also has space for shoes.

Materials List for Towel or Blanket Rack

2 ends	$1 \times 12 \times 38$ (or $3/4$ plywood)
2 handles	$1 \times 2 \times 13$
4 rails	36×1 diameter
2 rails	42×1 diameter

other two long enough to go through the ends and into the handles, leaving gaps about 1½ inch (FIG. 5-10C).

When you assemble, leave the handles until last. You may prefer to leave the extending rails too long and trim them to length after the other parts have determined the spacing of the ends.

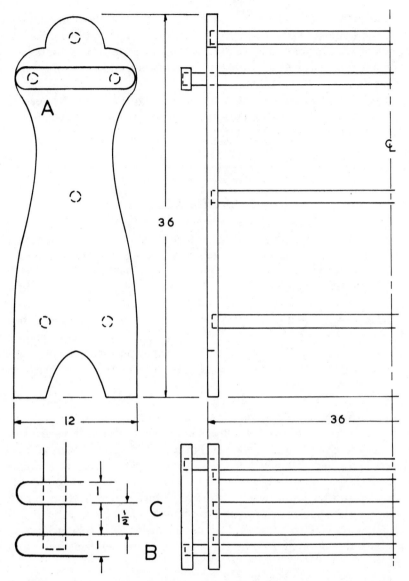

Fig. 5-10. *Sizes of the towel or blanket rack.*

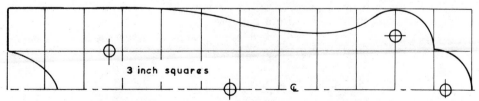

3 inch squares

Fig. 5-11. *Details of the shaping of the towel or blanket rack ends.*

Glue all the rails in place. As you do this, check that the distance between the ends is the same at top and bottom and between front and rear edges. Compare diagonal measurements and leave the assembly on a flat surface for the glue to set.

Remove any surplus glue from the extending rail ends. Trim them to the same length and glue on the handles.

For some situations you may prefer to leave the rails between the ends untreated, or only apply enough clear finish to seal the grain. Finish the ends with stain and polish or paint.

SHOE RACK

Without something to hold them together, a collection of shoes and boots can form an untidy pile. This rack (FIG. 5-12) is intended to hold a large number of shoes and boots on shelves. There is space for boots on the bottom shelf, then shoes may be put toe or heel first on two sloping shelves. High heels may hang over the front. The top shelf will accommodate more shoes or slippers, or it can be used for other things.

The sizes suggested (FIG. 5-13A) are intended to be for a rack to fit inside a clothes closet. You can alter then to suit your available space, but use the sizes for the shelf arrangements as a guide to suitable spacing for most shoes and boots. You may wish to check the sizes of your footwear if you need a special arrangement.

The main parts are ½-inch plywood, which will be best finished with paint. If you want a furniture-quality rack to stand in a room, you could use solid hardwood for a polished finish. If you use solid wood, you can have rabbets for the back and dado grooves for the shelves; but these techniques are unsatisfactory for plywood, and glued and nailed or screwed construction with cleats is shown (FIG. 5-14).

Prepare sufficient strip wood planed to ½-inch square section, for the joints.

Mark out the pair of sides, with the positions of all other parts (FIG. 5-13B and 5-14A). Allow for ⅛-inch hardboard behind all shelves and a ¾ inch piece of solid wood above the top shelf. Another strip will go across below near the front of the bottom shelf.

Put a strip on each side to take the back (FIG. 5-14B).

In front of this put the cleats to support the shelves. The top and bottom ones fit squarely (FIG. 5-14C) and the others slope (FIG. 5-14D), but all visible cleats have their front ends cut back. Round the exposed edges of the cleats. Make the bottom cleat short enough to admit the front crossbar.

Round the front top corners of the sides and cut away below the bottom cleats to form feet. See that the sides match as a pair.

Make the shelves all the same length with the ends cut back to fit around the fronts of the sides (FIG. 5-13C). They look best if the overlaps stop about ⅛ inch from the outside edges.

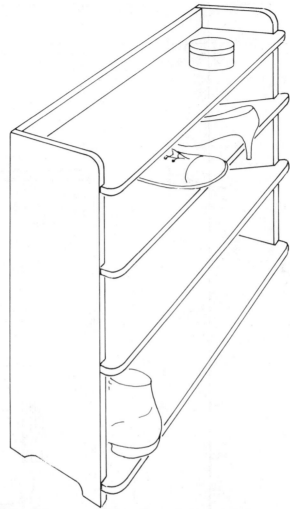

Fig. 5-12. This rack stores shoes on flat and sloping shelves.

Top and bottom shelves are cut squarely, but the other two shelves should be cut to match the slopes (FIG. 5-14E). Round the front corners and all exposed edges of the shelves.

Prepare the strip to go under the bottom shelf (FIG. 5-14F).

Assemble the shelves to the ends starting from the bottom up. Besides glue, use nails or screws to the cleats. When you fit the bottom shelf, join in the strip below as well.

After all shelves have been fitted, cut and fit the hardboard back (FIG. 5-14G). Stop its bottom edge about ½ inch above the floor.

Fit the strip at the back above the top shelf (FIG. 5-14H), gluing it to the shelf

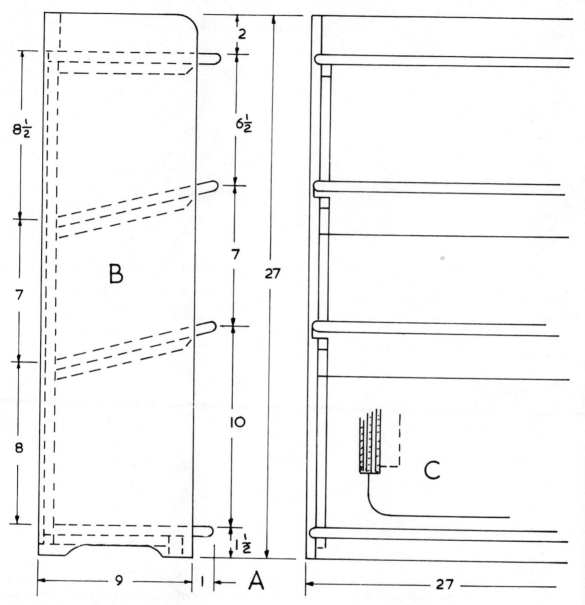

Fig. 5-13. Sizes of the shoe rack.

and placing screws or nails through the sides of the cabinet into the ends of the strips.

Make sure the rack will stand level. Remove any sharp edges and finish the wood with paint.

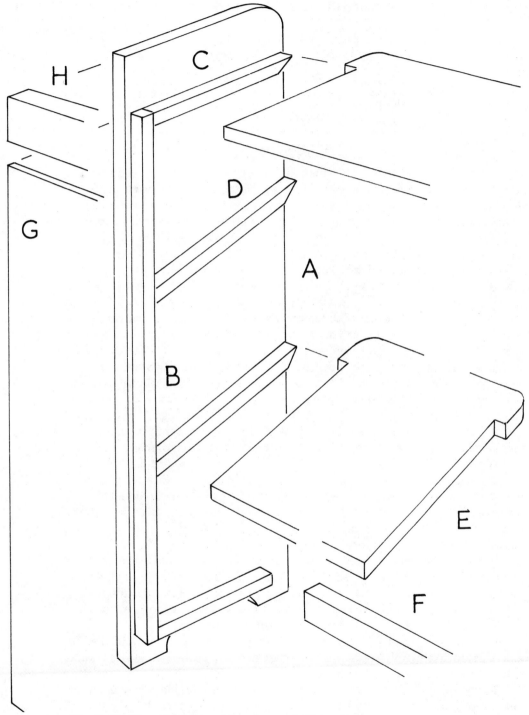

Fig. 5-14. How the parts of the shoe rack fit together.

Materials List for Shoe Rack

2 sides	$9 \times 27 \times \frac{1}{2}$ plywood
4 shelves	$10 \times 27 \times \frac{1}{2}$ plywood
1 back	$25 \times 27 \times \frac{1}{8}$ hardboard
1 bottom	$\frac{3}{4} \times 1 \times 27$
1 top	$\frac{3}{4} \times 2 \times 27$
8 cleats	$\frac{1}{2} \times \frac{1}{2} \times 10$
2 cleats	$\frac{1}{2} \times \frac{1}{2} \times 25$

BREAK-FRONT BOOKCASE

Books come in all sizes. That may be one of their attractions, but it makes designing difficult when you want to make a bookcase. If you measure the books you have and might have, arriving at bookcase sizes becomes bewildering. If you arrange shelves to provide clearance for large books, you waste space when most of the books are much smaller. It is difficult to arrive at a satisfactory compromise in a fixed-size bookcase.

One way of accommodating large and small books is to divide the bookcase into two sections, where the upper part is shallower and has closer shelves. This is compact and wastes less space. It may be called a break-front bookcase. That still leaves the problem of books of different heights which can be taken care of by making the shelves adjustable. This break-front bookcase (FIG. 5-15) has a lower section 11 inches deep and an upper section 8 inches deep. The shelves in each section can be moved up and down in $1\frac{1}{2}$ inch stages. The two units may be separated for ease of transport. The wide counter between the sections gives you somewhere to put books when removing and replacing them. If you can spare the space, the section over the counter could be left for other things than books.

If the whole bookcase is too much work for one weekend or you do not require all the shelving immediately, you can make the bottom part as one project and add the other part later.

The sizes suggested (FIG. 5-16) show a total height of 6 feet, with the counter at half that. The width could be anything you wish, but it is shown 30 inches. You may wish to measure your books of less common sizes. Some large books may need shelves wider than specified, and you may have to adapt sizes, but those shown should suit the majority of books.

Use a furniture-quality hardwood. The main parts should finish not less than $\frac{7}{8}$-inch thick. Books are heavy, and a thin shelf which seems adequate at first may develop a sag after a few months. Most of the joints may be doweled, although in places where they will be covered, you could use screws. The top part has dry dowels to fit into holes in the counter, so it can be lifted off.

Mark out the pair of sides for the lower unit (FIGS. 5-16A and 5-17A). Rabbet the rear edges to take the plywood back. There are two rails at the top (FIGS. 5-16B and 5-17B). Mark the position of the bottom shelf (FIG. 5-17C).

The two shelves (FIG. 5-16C) are 1 inch narrower than the sides and will rest on pull-out dowels fitting into holes in the sides (FIG. 5-17D). Mark the positions of these holes (FIG. 5-17E).

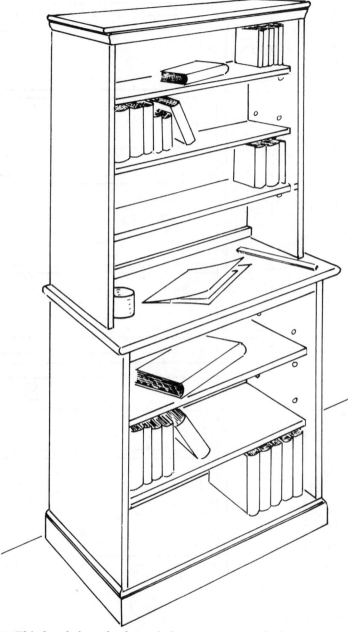

Fig. 5-15. This break-front bookcase is in two parts to take large and small books, as well as provide a working surface.

The holes need only be arranged over the area you expect to have to adjust. Shelves are unlikely to be needed nearer than 9 inches from the top or bottom, so mark accordingly. Delay drilling until you are ready to match shelves.

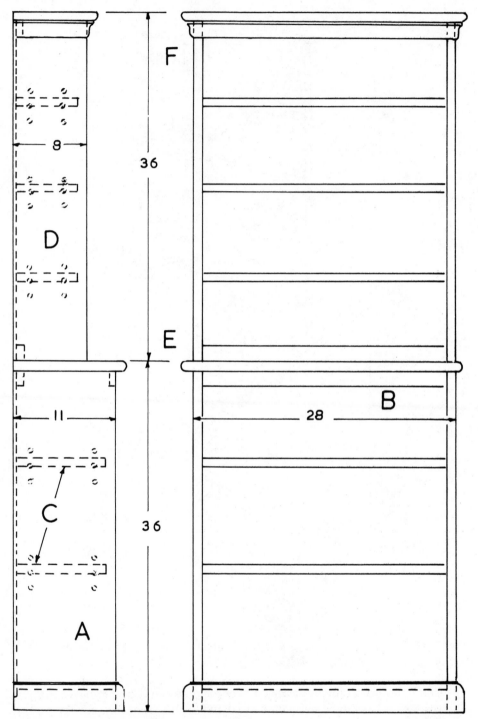

Fig. 5-16. Sizes of the break-front bookcase.

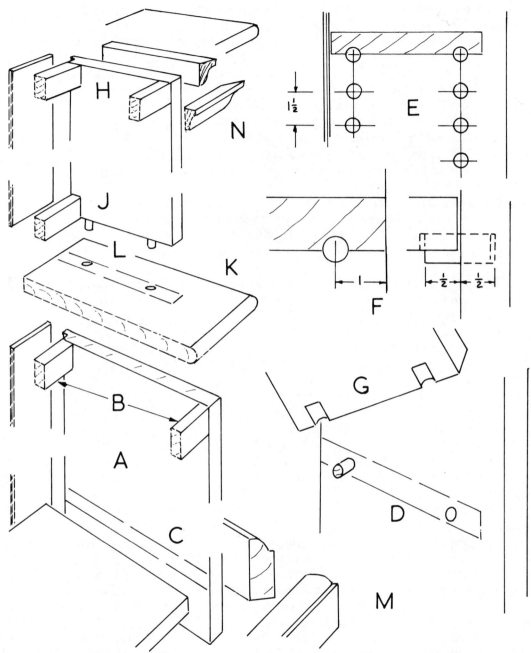

Fig. 5-17. Details of construction of the break-front bookcase and the method of arranging adjustment of shelves.

Mark the bottom shelf and the two top rails. Their lengths set the size of the bookcase. Prepare the ends for dowels into the sides. Two ½-inch dowels in each rail end, and three or four in the shelf should be adequate. As the plinth would cover screw heads, you could screw the ends of the shelf.

Make the two moveable shelves up to ⅛ inch shorter than the other crosswise parts. Mark the ends for the half holes to match those marked on the sides. Arrange them 1 inch from each edge of the shelf (FIG. 5-17F).

The dowels should have neatly squared ends and all be the same length. The holes in the case sides should allow a push fit, although having to grip with pliers is preferable to a very loose fit. The half holes may be a loose fit. If the dowels are exactly ½ inch and you have a 9/16 inch bit, that would be satisfactory for the half holes (FIG. 5-17G).

You could use a Forstner bit to drill the half holes, but the safest way of getting the half holes right, with this or any other bit, is to clamp a piece of scrap wood across the shelf end and drill centrally into the meeting surfaces. It will probably be advisable to experiment on spare pieces of wood before dealing with the shelves.

Have the plywood for the back ready. Join the sides with the bottom shelf and top rails. Glue and nail or screw the back into its rabbets and to the shelf edge and rear rail. The plywood need not reach the floor. It is sufficient to take it a little way below the shelf edge.

Except for removing surplus glue and testing the action of the inside shelves, do not do any further work on this part until the top unit has been assembled to the same stage.

Mark out and rabbet the sides of the upper unit (FIG. 5-16D) in a similar way to the lower sides. Allow for three shelves. There are two rails at the top (FIG. 5-17H) and one at the rear edge of the bottom (FIG. 5-17J).

Cut the rails to the same length as those of the lower unit. Make and drill the moveable shelves in a similar way to the lower ones.

Assemble the sides with the three rails and the plywood back, which should reach to the edges of the rails.

Make the counter top (FIG. 5-16E and 5-17K). At the back it covers the plywood. At front and sides, it extends about 1 inch with a rounded edge. You could work a molded edge, but in this position, where you are concerned with useful space and an edge which will be frequently knocked, a simple rounding is better.

Prepare the top edges of the lower unit for dowels into the counter. You could drive screws downwards into the rear rail and in the parts that will also be covered by the sides of the upper unit. A 6-inch spacing of screws or dowels would be satisfactory. Join the counter to the lower unit.

Drill each side of the upper unit for two ½-inch dowels (FIG. 5-17L) into the counter directly above the sides of the lower unit. Glue the dowels into the sides, but taper their ends slightly to go easily into dry holes in the counter top.

Make a plinth to go around the bottom edge of the lower unit, with its top edge level with the bottom shelf. This could be made with a simple beveled outer

Materials List for Break-front Bookcase

2 lower sides	$7/8 \times$	11×38
1 bottom shelf	$7/8 \times$	$10^3/4 \times 28$
2 rails	$7/8 \times$	2×28
2 shelves	$7/8 \times$	$9^3/4 \times 28$
1 plinth	$7/8 \times$	3×32
2 plinths	$7/8 \times$	3×13
1 counter top	$7/8 \times$	$12^1/2 \times 32$
2 upper sides	$7/8 \times$	8×38
3 rails	$7/8 \times$	2×28
3 shelves	$7/8 \times$	$6^3/4 \times 28$
2 backs	$28 \times$	$36 \times 1/4$ plywood
1 molding	$1 \times$	2×32
2 moldings	$1 \times$	2×13

edge or you could mold it. Miter the meeting corners (FIG. 5-17M). Glue it in place, using a few pins if necessary.

The top of the bookcase looks good with a crown molding around the edge of the front and sides, with the top board overhanging it. You could omit the molding, if you wish, for a simpler appearance. Make or buy the molding before shaping the top (FIG. 5-16F and 5-17N).

Cut and miter the molding to fit around the top in the same way as the plinth.

Make the top to cover the plywood at the back and overhang the molding with a projecting rounded edge.

Try all parts together, particularly the alternative positions of shelves. Do any necessary sanding, then finish with stain and polish or whatever other way you choose to match other furniture.

TILTING MAGAZINE RACK

Many magazine racks stand with their tops open so the contents have an untidy appearance. This rack (FIG. 5-18) has the magazines, books, and newspapers in a two part rack which is underneath a small tabletop when out of use, but if a latch is released, the rack can be tilted either way to allow access to half the contents. The same rack could be used for knitting or sewing items.

The suggested sizes (FIG. 5-19) are enough to accommodate plenty of magazines and folded newspapers. The top is large enough for drinks and other things you may want beside your chair. The ends include handles, so the rack can be moved easily.

Although you could use solid wood throughout, it may be easier to make some parts of plywood. If this is hardwood plywood, with matching solid wood parts, you can stain and polish the rack. With softwood plywood and most other parts softwood, you can finish the rack with paint.

The assembly consists of an outer stand and the inner tilting rack, which are made separately. It will be simplest to make the stand first, then use it as a guide to

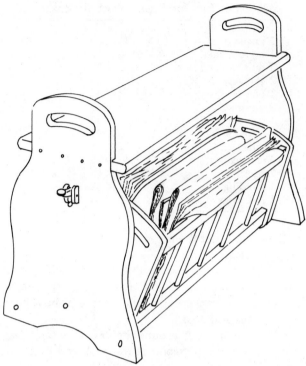

Fig. 5-18. *This magazine rack is arranged to tilt either way for easy access to the contents.*

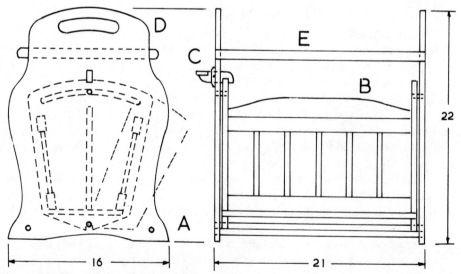

Fig. 5-19. *Sizes of the tilting magazine rack.*

sizes of the rack. The function of the whole rack should be understood first. The outer part consists of the handled ends joined with the tabletop and three lower rods (FIG. 5-19A). The rack has a central division between two rodded sides, all joined to the ends which pivot on the central bottom round rod (FIG. 5-19B). To keep the rack upright, there is a latch through one end (FIG. 5-19C). When this is released, the rack may be tilted either way, and the movement is limited by a stop in a slot at both ends.

Cut the ends of the stand first (FIG. 5-19D). Use the half drawing (FIG. 5-20A) to get the shape and positions of holes. Round the outer edges, except the feet, and round the edges of the hand holes. Do not cut the latch slot yet, but you can drill for the three rods (FIG. 5-21A). These can be ½-inch hardwood dowel rods. If you are doubtful about the stiffness of available rods, increase their size to ⅝ inch diameter.

Make the tabletop from solid wood (FIGS. 5-19E and 5-21B). Cut it to fit closely around the ends. Round the outer edges and corners. Mark and drill for ¼-inch dowels in all parts. Use dowels to make a dry assembly of the stand, so you can use it to get sizes of the rack. You will have to disassemble it later to fit the latch and the stop pegs.

Cut the two ends of the tilting rack (FIG. 5-21C) using the half drawing (FIG. 5-20B) to get the outline and positions of mortises and slots. Cut the central notch (FIG. 5-20C) in the top edge of one piece only. If possible, use a compass with its point at the center of the hole which will go over the supporting rod to get the curve of the slot and top edge. The bottom notch must fit the supporting rod on the stand. Do not cut the mortises yet.

You have to make the rack to fit easily between the ends of the stand. There can be up to ¼-inch clearance. Cut the central division, with an overall length to suit. Cut tenons to match the mortises marked on the ends (FIG. 5-21D and 5-22A). Shape the top edge (FIG. 5-22B) and round it. Cut the mortises in the rack ends to match, so bottom edges will be level.

Prepare the strips for top and bottom of the sides (FIG. 5-21E). They are the same overall length as the central division, but with the ends reduced to form tenons (FIG. 5-22C). Bevel the undersides of the bottom strips to suit the angle of the ends. Drill all strips to make ⅜-inch rods (FIG. 5-22D), going halfway through. Take sharpness off all edges which will be exposed.

The latch has to be fitted through one end so it will engage with a notch in the trough (FIG. 5-23A). Put the trough end with the lower notch on the supporting rod of the stand, and check its position in relation to the slot marked on the stand end. You may have to adjust the marking on the stand end to get the slot at the right height.

Make the latch (FIG. 5-23B) from hardwood, even if the rest of the magazine rack is softwood. Fit a flat piece across the end. This is shown round (FIG. 5-23C), but it could be square or any other shape. Do not make it very heavy, as the greater weight should be the other side of the pivot, then the latch does not accidentally rise out of the notch.

Cut the slot in the stand end so the latch will swing up clear of the notch. Put

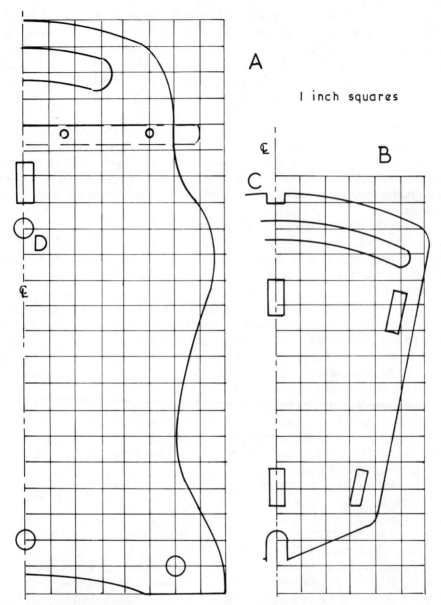

Fig. 5-20. Shapes of the end parts of the tilting magazine rack.

a strip at each side of the slot to take the pivot rod, which may be a piece of stout nail or any wire up to ³⁄₁₆-inch diameter. Glue and screw on the strips. Drill for the pivot and try the action.

At both stand ends there have to be stops made from short pieces of dowel rod (FIG. 5-20D) projecting through the slots in the rack ends (FIG. 5-23D). Check the

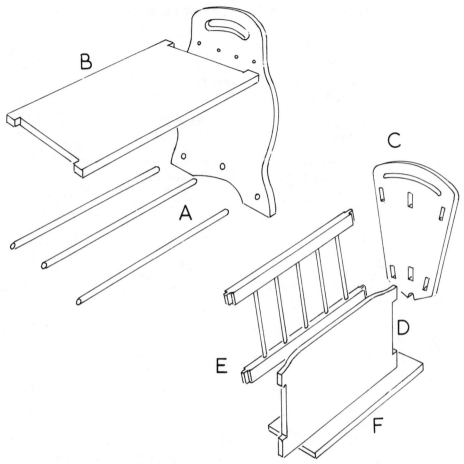

Fig. 5-21. Assembly details of parts of the tilting magazine rack.

positions of the holes and drill to take the pegs. Try the swing of each end with the peg in position. Ease the slots, if necessary, so movement to the limit is smooth both ways.

Separate the parts of the stand. Do any final sanding, then glue them together. The dowels that hold the top may be allowed to project slightly until after gluing, then they can be sanded level to show as decorative features.

Glue the dowel rods into the side strips of the tilting rack, then glue the central partition and the side strips into the rack ends. See that this assembly is square. Add a bottom (FIG. 5-21F) with glue and screws. When the glue has set, remove any excess glue, level the outside edges and round all exposed corners.

Try the tilting rack in place in the stand, with temporary stop pegs fitted. Make any final adjustments. Test the action of the latch and fit it with its pivot rod.

Apply a finish before finally assembling with glued stop pegs.

Materials List for Tilting Magazine Rack

½ inch plywood	
2 stand ends	16 × 23
2 rack ends	12 × 16
1 rack division	10 × 20
1 rack bottom	39 × 20
solid wood	
1 top	⅝ × 14 × 22
4 rack sides	¾ × 1½ × 20
10 side rods	8 × ⅜ diameter
3 bottom rods	22 × ½ diameter
top dowels, from	12 × ¼ diameter
latch, from	¼ × 1 × 6

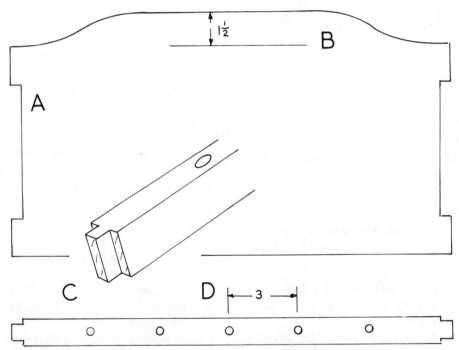

Fig. 5-22. Division and rails for the tilting magazine rack.

BED HEAD

A divan-type bed may be bought and used without a headboard, but it is better with something at the head. This could be a board or part of an arrangement of shelves and cabinets attached to the wall, but if you want the head or board to be part of the bed, it can be made to be attached. This bed head (FIG. 5-24) bolts to

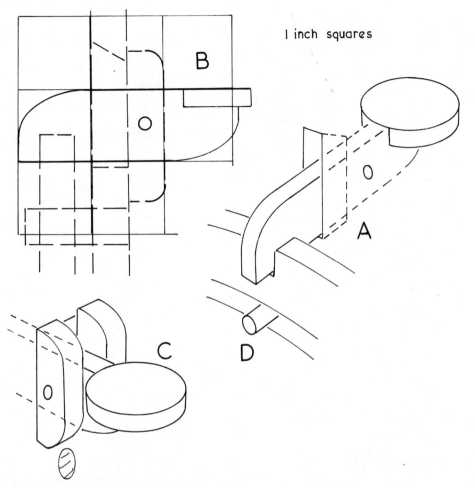

1 inch squares

Fig. 5-23. The catch for securing the tilting magazine rack.

the end of the bed and can be adjusted for height. It is easily removed if ever necessary.

Two designs of similar size are suggested. One has all flat parts. The other is basically the same, but uses some turned parts. The first design would look well in softwood, if other furniture has to be matched. Although the second design could be softwood, turning is better done in hardwood, and the effect of polished turned hardwood is visually more pleasing.

The head could be made to suit a bed of any width. It is drawn as if for one 48 inches wide. The number and spacing of uprights may be adjusted to suit other widths. The flat slat arrangement looks best if the gaps between slats are slightly wider than the slats. The turned spindles could be at any spacing, but turning them to match exactly may be a little difficult, and a wider spacing does not allow such a close comparison!

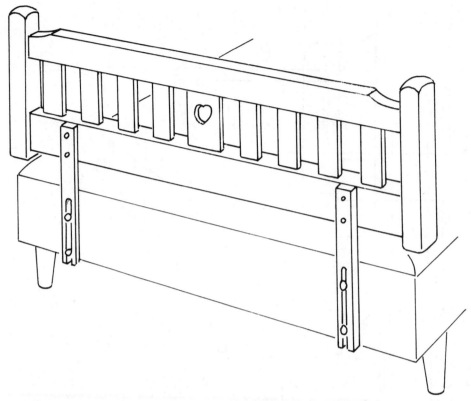

Fig. 5-24. This bed head is designed for attaching to an existing bed.

Mortise and tenon joints are suggested for most parts, but you could use dowels. They should be between one-third and one-half the thickness of the wood in diameter and not less than two in each joint. Tenons and dowels should penetrate between ½ inch and ¾ inch.

Instructions are given first for the bed head with flat parts, then differences are shown if the turned parts are chosen.

Prepare wood for the top (FIG. 5-25A) and bottom (FIG. 5-25B) rails, allowing sufficient at the ends for tenons, if that is the method of assembly to be used.

Mark out the two together with the positions of the slats. Mark the ends for the lengths of the tenons. Cut down the ends of the top rail (FIG. 5-25C) to 2 inches from 4 inches long.

Mark out the slats (FIG. 5-25D) together. There could be 2-inch slats for the whole width, but a 4-inch one with a heart cutout (FIG. 5-25E and 5-26A) is suggested. Allow for tenons or dowels at the ends.

Cut tenons (FIG. 5-25F) or drill for dowels (FIG. 5-25G) and prepare matching mortises or holes in the rails.

The two square end posts extend above and below the other parts. Mark them out (FIG. 5-26B), using the slats to get the vertical positions to match.

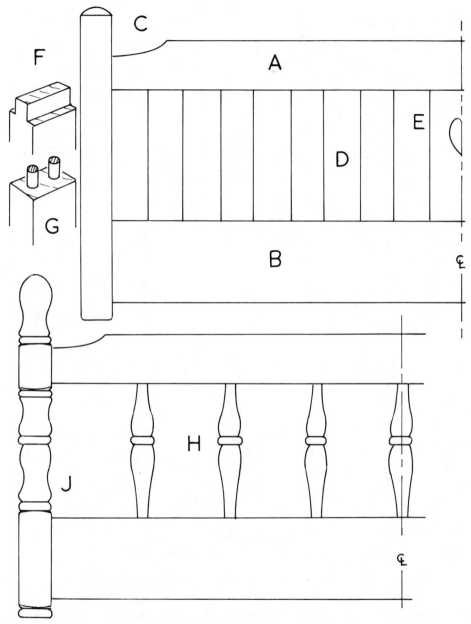

Fig. 5-25. Alternative bed head designs using flat or turned parts.

Take the sharpness off the extending corners at the bottom and dome the tops (FIG. 5-26C).

Cut mortise and tenon joints between the rails and the posts. They can be single at the top (FIG. 5-26D), but it would be better to use double tenons at the bottom rail (FIG. 5-26E).

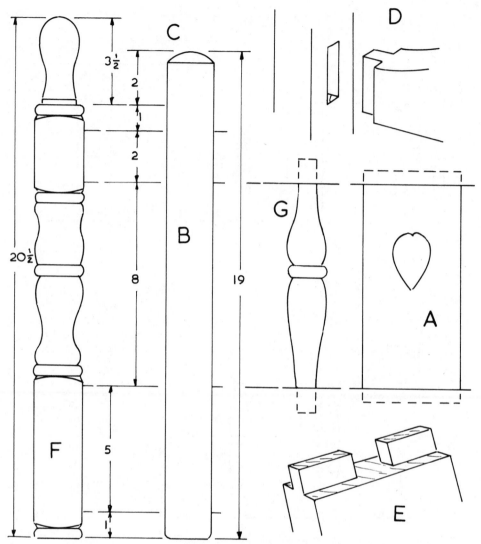

Fig. 5-26. Parts for making the bed head in alternative forms.

Before assembly, lightly round edges of all parts. Sanding will be easier and more effective now than if you leave it until after assembly.

Assemble the slats to the rails first, then the rails to the posts. Check squareness by comparing diagonal measurements.

If you wish to use turned spindles and posts, start by marking out the rails together, with the positions of the spindle holes, which can be drilled ¾-inch diameter. Mark the ends of the rails for tenons or dowels.

Mark the posts (FIG. 5-26F), allowing for some extra at the ends for mounting in the lathe. The wood will be square to a little above and below the rail positions, but the other parts are round.

Materials List for Bed Head (for 48-inch bed)

1 top rail	$1\frac{1}{4} \times 3 \times 48$
1 bottom rail	$1\frac{1}{4} \times 5 \times 48$
2 supports	$1 \times 2 \times 18$
Flat parts	
2 posts	$2 \times 2 \times 20$
1 slat	$1 \times 4 \times 12$
8 slats	$1 \times 2 \times 12$
Turned parts	
2 posts	$2 \times 2 \times 22$
7 spindles	$1\frac{1}{2} \times 1\frac{1}{2} \times 12$

You may use your own ideas for the turned pattern, but the posts and spindles are shown with beads just above the center of the distance between the rails (FIG. 5-26H). This looks better than exactly central.

Turn the two posts (FIG. 5-25J and 5-26F). Mark and cut the mortise and tenon or dowel joints with the rails.

Turn the spindles (FIGS. 5-25H and 5-26G) with beads that will come in line with those of the posts, and ends to fit in the rail holes. There can be a little tolerance in the lengths of the spindles and the depths of the holes, so during assembly spindles can be moved up and down to get all beads in line.

Take sharpness off all square edges and do any necessary sanding, then glue the spindles into their holes and the rails to the posts in one operation, so spindle positions can be adjusted, if necessary, before the glue has set.

Give the wood your chosen finish, probably to match surrounding furniture.

How the bed head is mounted on the bed end depends on the bed arrangement. One method is suggested (FIG. 5-24). There may be already two sets of bolts in the bed end. If not, you can drill for them a short distance in from the sides — $3/8$-inch bolts would be suitable. Drill for two bolts in the bottom rail of the bed head to match their positions. You could use carriage bolts with their round heads at the front, where they would be inconspicuous, or you may prefer to just use screws from the back.

The two uprights may be a 1-inch $\times$ 2-inch strip, drilled to match the bolts and support the head at a suitable height. If you want to make the height adjustable, cut long slots, as shown, and use large washers under the nuts or bolt heads.

PLAYPEN

One of the best ways of keeping a young child within bounds is with a playpen. It allows a crawling child to play with toys, but mother knows he is restricted in his movements to a fairly small area. One problem is concerned with space. You want to give the child enough room to play, yet the whole assembly must not be so big that it causes an obstruction; then when it is out of use, you need to reduce its size as much as possible.

This playpen (FIG. 5-27) is about 40 inches square and 24 inches high. It has a base which protects the floor and prevents an energetic child from moving the pen about, as well as keeping the pen in shape. For folding, the two-part base is removed, then the framework folds flat to a total thickness of about 6 inches.

Most of the uprights are ½-inch hardwood dowel rods. You may wish to obtain them first, so you can cut stock lengths most economically, as slight differences in height will not matter. The framework could be softwood, but choose a straight-grained type that is unlikely to splinter. A better, although heavier, pen would be made with hardwood. If you can match the framework and dowel wood, then give a clear finish, the pen will look attractive in any room. Alternatively, softwood may be finished with paint.

It is important that parts match and the assembled frameworks are square. To secure accuracy, mark all parts that should be the same together. Compare parts as you make them. If pairs of parts are not quite the same both ways, mark them so they go together the better way. You can use a try square across batches of rails to

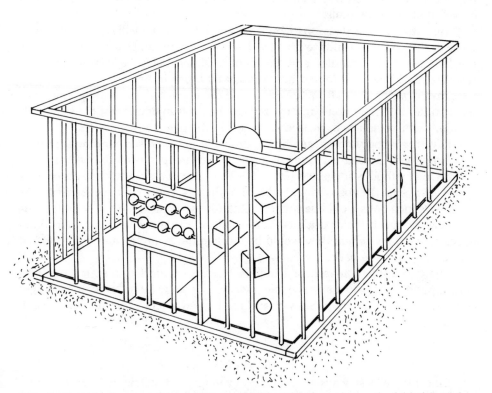

Fig. 5-27. This playpen which will keep a child within bounds may be folded flat when out of use.

transfer lengths and hole spacings. Mark each hole position with crossing lines, then use a fine punch to provide a starting place for the bit.

Prefabricate as far as possible, before assembling. Make and match the opposite long sides, then prepare the folding sides. The design shown (FIG. 5-28) has uprights spaced 4 inches apart. This is close enough for a child to be unable to get his head through. If you alter sizes, do not exceed this spacing, and be careful at the corners that the diagonal spacing there does not become excessive.

Mark out the four long rails (FIG. 5-28A and B). On one side allow for two square uprights to support the bead rails, but on the opposite side you could repeat this arrangement or have round rods all the way.

Mark out the four folding sides (FIG. 5-28C).

Drill all holes. Use a stop on the drill or press and go about three-quarters of the way through (FIG. 5-29A).

Where the square posts are to come (FIG. 5-28D) prepare for two 1/4-inch dowels at each position (FIG. 5-29B).

Cut the square posts to length and mark on the positions of the short crossbars (FIG. 5-28E), which are joined with dowels in the same way as the posts to the main rails and have holes for upright rods. Cut one or more pieces of scrap wood to the same length as the square posts to act as jigs during assembly (FIG. 5-29C).

The beads slide on rods set into holes in the uprights (FIG. 5-28F). The rods should be stiff enough to resist any possibility of a child bending them. A diameter of 3/16 inch would be suitable. If you buy colored wood or plastic beads, you will probably have to enlarge the holes to slide easily on the rods. Include the metal rods and beads as you assemble the short rails to their uprights.

Glue the uprights in place. It is important that the assembled heights of all frames are the same. Use the jig to maintain the correct distances as you assemble parts (FIG. 5-29D). It will help to prevent parts moving before the glue has set if pins are driven across end joints (FIG. 5-29E).

Remove excess glue and take sharpness off all edges.

The frames have to be assembled so the short parts fold inwards between the long parts (FIG. 5-28G). Use butt hinges the full depth of the wood. If possible, get hinges with broad arms and a good spread of screw holes. Arrange the short frames to extend over the ends of the long frames (FIG. 5-28H). There is no need to let the hinges into the wood, as their thickness on the surfaces will provide clearance during folding. Assemble the frames and check the folding and extending action.

Materials List for Playpen

4 rails	$1 \times 1\frac{1}{2} \times 42$
8 rails	$1 \times 1\frac{1}{2} \times 22$
2 rails	$1 \times 1\frac{1}{2} \times 13$
2 uprights	$1 \times 1\frac{1}{2} \times 24$
38 uprights	$25 \times \frac{1}{2}$ diameter

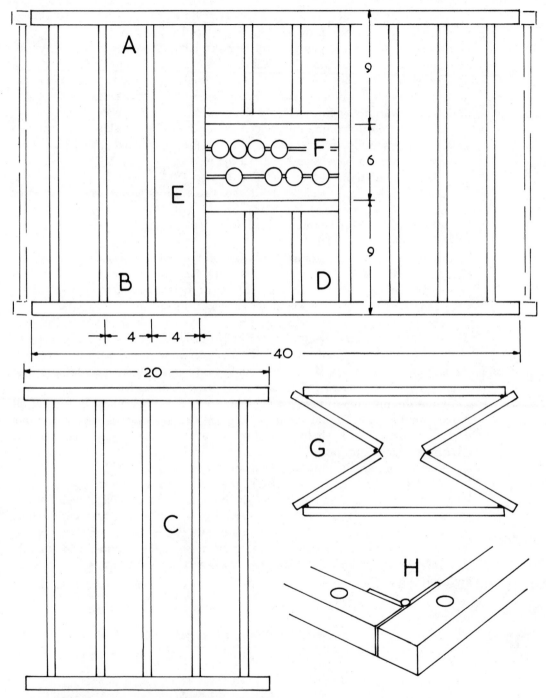

Fig. 5-28. Sizes and methods of folding the playpen.

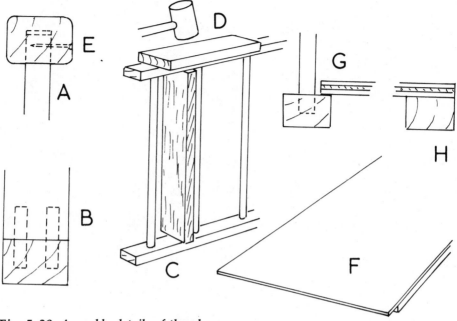

Fig. 5-29. Assembly details of the playpen.

Make the base with two pieces of plywood that meet across the center of the pen (FIG. 5-29F). Cut them to size to rest on the bottom rails and come close to the round uprights (FIG. 5-29G). Notch loosely around the square uprights. Put strips under the meeting edges (FIG. 5-29H) at the same height as the rails and short enough to fit between them. With the two parts of the base in position, the playpen should be held rigidly in shape, so the assembly forms a safe unit that cannot move whatever its young occupant does.

Finish the framework with varnish or polish. The base may be left untreated or given a matt paint finish. It should not be glossy.

6

Containers

In every home, a great many things accumulate, such as papers, clothing, equipment, food, and even outright trash, which need to be kept in groups and stored neatly to create tidy rooms and the ability to find things when you want them.

Some things may best be stored on racks, but most items may be better put in boxes. Papers, pens and what you need for writing or drawing require a desktop container. If you have to dispose of scrap paper or other material, the container can be an open box or bin. For many household items it is better to have some sort of cabinet or cupboard with drawers. If you have children, there may be the problem of looking after toys, and containers will help avoid confusion and messy storage.

For a home that is somewhat fully furnished, the weekend woodworker may exercise his skills best by creating containers of many sorts to improve his family's convenience and comfort. Most homes will benefit by the addition of more containers and, within obvious limits, cannot have enough of them. The projects described in this chapter may provide ideas for you to modify to suit your needs, if the designs as offered are not quite what you want.

TAPERED BIN

Boxes or bins may have many purposes. They can be used for waste in an office or shop. They have similar uses in kitchen, bathroom or bedroom. They can contain produce such as vegetables in a garden shed or other storeroom. Sizes may vary according to needs. It is an advantage if a bin is tapered, so the contents may be tipped out easily. This is such a bin (FIG. 6-1). The sizes suggested (FIG. 6-2) are for bins that would be useful in an office or shop. You may reduce sizes for

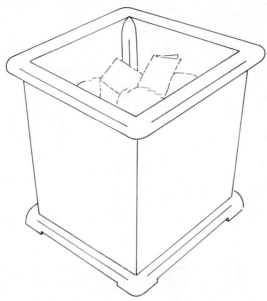

Fig. 6-1. This tapered bin can be used for waste materials or other things and is easy to empty.

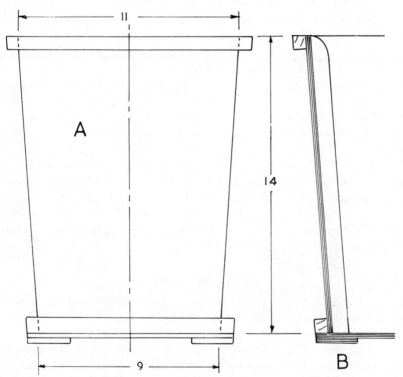

Fig. 6-2. Sizes of the tapered bin.

bedroom or bathroom, but you might want larger bins for vegetables. Besides the top rim's use for stiffening, it provides a grip for lifting.

Construction is with ¼-inch plywood panels, although you might consider using hardboard, which should be strong enough for careful use. Framing is with solid wood strips. For a painted finish these could be softwood. If you use attractive hardwood panels, the strips could match for a polished finish. Assembly is with glue and pins. If you expect any of the contents to be moist, use a waterproof glue. The whole bin should then be as watertight as a bucket.

In a squared tapered construction, which is part of a cone, corner angles will not be exactly square in the cross-section of the wood. If there is much slope the angle between the outside surfaces will be more obtuse than 90°. In this bin the slope is only slight and the difference is negligible, and if noticeable, can be taken care of by planing when fitting.

Cut four side panels (FIG. 6-2A) and check that they are identical and symmetrical.

Construction could be by adding strips to two opposite sides and joining them with the other parts, but you can make all four sides the same before joining. Make the corner strips with curved tops and lower ends a little too long (FIG. 6-3A). Attach them to the same edge on all four panels.

Add strips across the outside at top and bottom (FIG. 6-3B and H). At the side with the inside strip, they project enough to cover the plywood. At the other side leave more than enough to overlap the adjoining strip, so you can cut level after assembly.

Bring these assemblies together in turn and glue and pin the corners. Cut the bottoms of the corner strips level.

Have the plywood bottom (FIG. 6-3D) ready and glue and pin it on. This will hold the lower part of the bin square, but check that the top edges are also square.

When the glue has set trim off any excess wood.

Put 2-inch-square feet (FIG. 6-2B and 6-3E) under the corners

For shop or garden use you may be satisfied with square edges and corners or minimal rounding, but for indoor use the bin looks better and is more convenient if the outer corners are well rounded and all edges are slightly rounded.

Apply the chosen finish. For food you may leave the inside bare or give it a coat of paint or varnish that is safe with food, but for most purposes apply paint, varnish, or polish all over.

Materials List for Tapered Bin

4 panels	11 × 14 × ¼ plywood
1 bottom	11 × 11 × ¼ plywood
4 feet	2 × 2 × ¼ plywood
4 corners	¾ × ¾ × 16
4 top edges	⅝ × ⅝ × 15
4 bottom edges	⅝ × ⅝ × 13

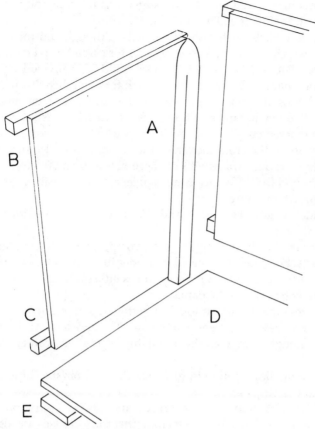

Fig. 6-3. Assembly of the tapered bin.

ESCRITOIRE

In many homes there is a need for some office facilities for dealing with domestic correspondence and accounts, yet a complete desk might take up more room than would be justified. This unit, with a rather ambitious name, can be placed at the back of a side table to convert it into a temporary desk. It is intended to store the usual office requirements and records, while having a pleasing appearance (FIG. 6-4). It is not designed for attachment to the table and should not be too heavy to move about, if you expect to have more than one work place.

Sizes are not critical and you may wish to modify them to suit a particular table or situation. The drawing (FIG. 6-5) shows divisions about 12 inches wide, which will give clearance to most papers, booklets and similar things you may wish to put away. If you want to make your escritoire narrower, it would be advisable to keep the center compartment 12 inches wide, where there are two positions for holding paper and envelopes, with a space below for pens, pins and the many bits and pieces you accumulate. To the left there is a compartment with a

Fig. 6-4. This escritoire will convert a table into a desk.

shelf and a lift-out door about 12 inches square. This might be used as a drawing board, for cutting on or as a work surface for a hobby. At the other side is a drawer and a compartment behind double doors. Decorative pieces at top and sides relieve the plainness and cover the edges of a plywood back.

Any wood could be used. Softwood might be painted, but it would probably be better to use a hardwood to match existing furniture. The thin sloping divisions in the center could be plywood and you may use plywood or hardboard for the back. In its simplest form you could make the unit with nailed joints and disguise this construction with paint. For a better quality piece of furniture, several possible joints are suggested in the instructions.

In effect, you are making a box which will be stood on its side. Treat it as a box while laying out the outside and its divisions. Prepare the outside parts and get the sizes of the inside pieces from them. Decide on the corner joints you will use, as this will affect the lengths of parts to be cut. Exposed through dovetails would show your skill as a woodworker (FIG. 6-6A). If you have a suitable router cutter and jig, you could use half-blind dovetails (FIG. 6-6B). For a simpler joint you could rabbet one piece and use glue with pins both ways (FIG. 6-6C). If you want to use dowels, let the case ends extend upwards a small amount (FIG. 6-6D). In a counter-bored screwed joint, the plugs might be regarded as decoration (FIG. 6-6E).

Mark out the top and bottom (FIG. 6-5A and 6-7A) with allowance at the ends for the chosen joints and the positions of divisions.

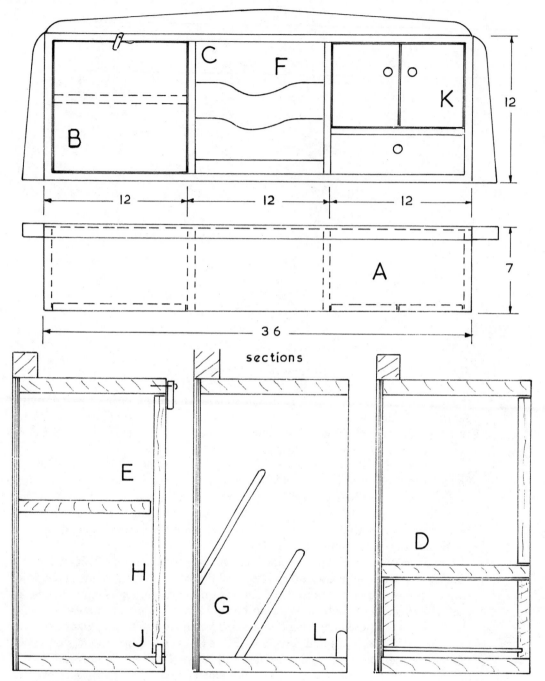

Fig. 6-5. Sizes and sections of the escritoire.

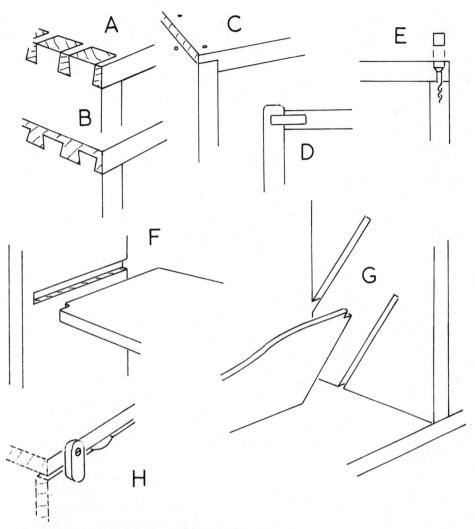

Fig. 6-6. Suggested joints for parts of the escritoire.

Prepare the ends to match (FIG. 6-5B and 6-7B). From these get the sizes of the upright divisions (FIG. 6-5C and 6-7C), allowing for their ends going into stopped dados (FIG. 6-6F).

Make the shelf over the drawer (FIG. 6-5D and 6-7D) the full width of the parts it joins and cut stopped dado joints.

The shelf at the other side has to be set back by the thickness of the door (FIG. 6-5E and 6-7E). It will act as a stop for this lift-out door. Cut dado joints to suit.

The two paper divisions are the same width (FIG. 6-5F and 6-7F). Hollow the front edges and round them. Bevel the rear edges to fit against the bottom or the back (FIG. 6-5G). If you do not have facilities for cutting narrow grooves, you could

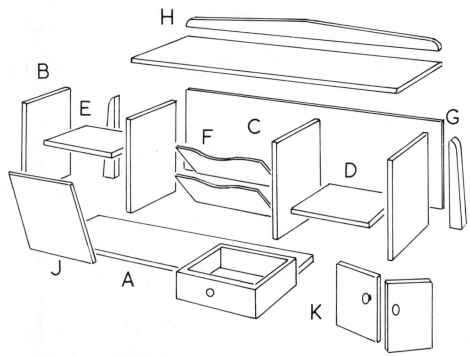

Fig. 6-7. How the parts of the escritoire fit together.

put a piece of wood about ⅜-inch thick between each end of the divisions and screw this to the uprights.

Check all parts made so far for size and whether the joints will fit, then glue and clamp them together. If you have the back plywood ready, you can screw that on to hold the other parts square. When the glue has set, remove any surplus glue and trim any excess wood at joints.

The outside decorative pieces are made from 1 inch × 2 inch wood. Taper the end pieces to 1 inch and round the tops (FIG. 6-7G). Taper the top piece from the center and round the ends similarly (FIG. 6-7H). Join these pieces to the unit with ⅜ inch dowels and glue—a 6-inch spacing should be adequate. Rear edges should be level with the outside of the back plywood.

Make the lift-out door (FIG. 6-5H and 6-7J) an easy fit in its opening. Have the grain upright. Put two ¼-inch dowels in the lower edge about 2 inches from each side (FIG. 6-4 and 6-5J). Drill matching holes in the bottom to allow the dowels to drop in easily.

The closed door will be stopped from going too far in by the shelf. Cut a shallow notch in the top of the door, for using a finger to pull it open, and make a small turnbutton to hold the door closed (FIG. 6-6H).

Make the pair of doors at the other side (FIG. 6-5K and 6-7K) to fit into the opening. Fit handles or knobs. You could use butt hinges set into the door edges or

Materials List for Escritoire

1 top	$5/8 \times 7 \times 38$
1 bottom	$5/8 \times 7 \times 38$
2 ends	$5/8 \times 7 \times 14$
2 divisions	$5/8 \times 7 \times 14$
1 shelf	$1/2 \times 6\frac{1}{4} \times 13$
1 shelf	$5/8 \times 7 \times 13$
1 back	$12 \times 38 \times 1/4$ plywood
1 back strip	$1 \times 2 \times 38$
2 back strips	$1 \times 2 \times 14$
2 paper divisions	$5 \times 13 \times 1/4$ plywood
1 door	$5/8 \times 12 \times 12$
2 doors	$5/8 \times 6 \times 8$
1 drawer front	$5/8 \times 3\frac{1}{2} \times 13$
2 drawer sides	$1/2 \times 3\frac{1}{2} \times 8$
1 drawer back	$1/2 \times 3 \times 13$
1 drawer bottom	$7 \times 12 \times 1/4$ plywood

ornamental hinges on the surface. Arrange magnetic catches under the top of the unit. If the catches do not act as stops, put a small block of wood on the shelf to prevent the doors going too far.

The drawer could be made fully dovetailed in the traditional way, or you might use a simpler construction. The front might overlap the sides with a rabbet (FIG. 6-6C), but with screws through the sides and no pins showing at the front. The drawer bottom should fit into grooves and the back could be screwed between the sides. Fit a knob or handle to match those on the doors.

Put a strip across the front of the center compartment (FIG. 6-5L) to retain anything you put there.

Finish in your preferred way. Glue cloth to the underside to prevent slipping or damaging a polished tabletop.

TOY BOX

When young children or parents accumulate toys, their storage becomes a problem. This box is a way of keeping smaller ones together. With its compartments and a sliding tray, the child is encouraged to put away toys in an orderly manner and to develop a system, so he can find what he wants. The casters and rope handles enable the child to move the box to where the toys are, and to gather them at the end of a play session.

The box (FIG. 6-8) is about the size of a blanket chest. You may wish to modify sizes to suit your needs, but the instructions are for a box 15 inches wide and deep and 30 inches long (FIG. 6-9A).

Construction is mainly with plywood panels stiffened with 3/4 inch square solid wood strips. There are no special joints to cut. If glue is used, it should be satisfactory to attach strips with nails at about 3-inch spacing, with screws at corner joints and anywhere where greater loads may be expected.

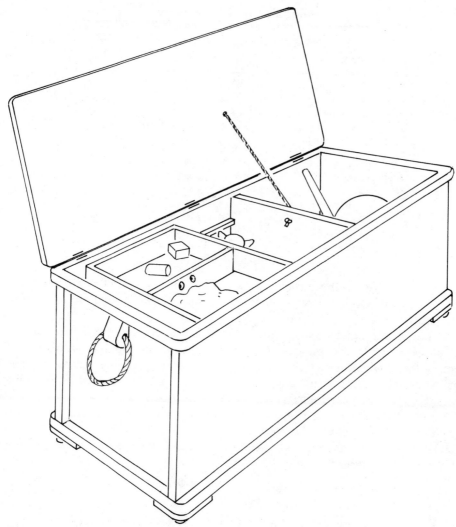

Fig. 6-8. This toy box will keep toys tidy and it can be moved about on casters.

Make two end assemblies (Figs. 6-9B and 6-10A). Top and bottom strips go across and the uprights are between them.

Cut the plywood for the two sides (Figs. 6-9C and 6-10B). Mark on the positions of the divisions and the runners (Fig. 6-9D).

Attach the ½-inch-square runners to the sides. Cut back enough to fit inside the end (Fig. 6-10C).

Put the outside stiffening strips on the top and bottom edges of the sides (Fig. 6-10D).

Make the two divisions the same width as the ends. The taller one should come within ½ inch of the top edge of a side (Fig. 6-10E). The lower one should be

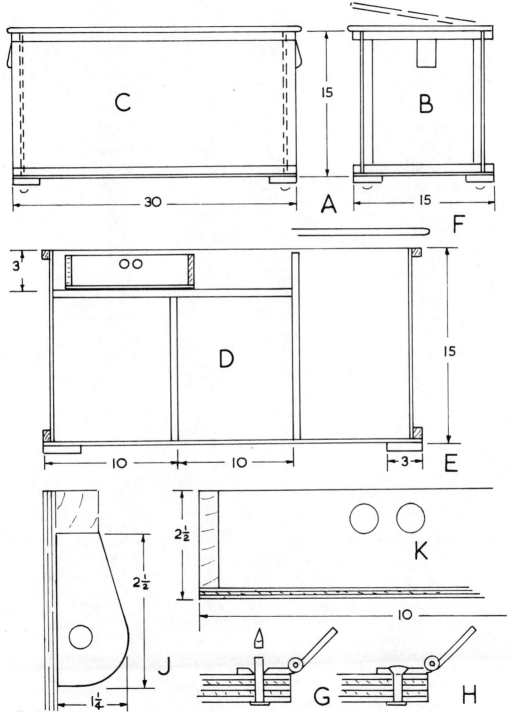

Fig. 6-9. Sizes and details of the toy box.

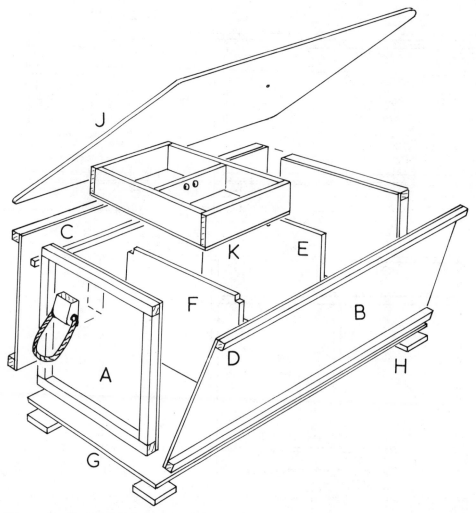

Fig. 6-10. *Fitting together parts of the toy box.*

notched to fit around the runners and should come to within about ⅛ inch of their top edges (FIG. 6-10F). Round the top edges of both divisions. Drill a hole ¾ inch down from the center of the top of the taller division to take the cord which will hold the opened lid. Lightly countersink both sides.

Join the sides to the ends and add the divisions.

Cut the bottom (FIG. 6-10G) slightly too large and attach it to the ends and sides to hold the assembly square. Plane the edges of the bottom level and add blocks under the corners (FIG. 6-9E and 6-10H), as attachment points for the casters or to serve as feet if you do not want casters.

Strengthen the top corners with screws driven from the stiffening strips on the sides into the stiffening strips on the ends.

Well round the corners of the stiffening strips, top and bottom. Take sharp edges off all around.

Cut the lid (FIG. 6-10J) to come level at the hinge side, but overhang ¼ inch at the ends and front (FIG. 6-9F). Round all edges and corners, except the hinged edge.

Use three hinges, which may be 2 inches long. If they are thin, it should be satisfactory to fit them without setting them in, but thick ones will be neater and cause less gap if the bottom leaf is set in.

Plywood ½-inch thick does not provide much grip for screws and it would be better to rivet the hinges to the lid. If you do not have suitable soft metal rivets, use copper nails. Drill and drive through each nail, then cut off its end (FIG. 6-9G), leaving enough to hammer into the countersunk hole of the hinge (FIG. 6-9H).

Drill a hole in the lid for the cord to match the position of the hole in the division. Countersink it slightly both sides. Colored braided cord about ³⁄₁₆-inch diameter would be suitable. Screw the hinges to the rear edge of the box.

Although softwood will be satisfactory for other parts of the box, the blocks for the rope loops are better made of a close-grained hardwood. Cut them to shape (FIG. 6-9J) 1½ inches thick and drill a hole for the rope, which may be about ³⁄₈-inch diameter. Attach the blocks with glue and three or four screws from inside.

The sliding tray (FIG. 6-10K) is a box, which may be made of solid wood or you could use cutoffs of ½-inch plywood. Nail or screw corners and add a ¼-inch plywood bottom. The division may have two finger holes for lifting and sliding (FIG. 6-9K).

A painted finish would be appropriate. A light color inside aids visibility. The outside could be darker, or you may choose pink for a girl and blue for a boy. You could add the child's name and other painted or decal decorations. Screw on furniture-type casters under the corners.

Materials List for Toy Box

(¼)	
2 ends	13 × 15
2 sides	15 × 30
1 bottom	15 × 30
1 tray bottom	10 × 13
½ inch plywood	
1 lid	15½ × 31
1 division	13 × 15
1 division	12 × 15
2 tray sides	2½ × 13
2 tray ends	2½ × 10
1 tray division	2½ × 9
4 feet, solid wood	3 × 3
8 end frames	¾ × ¾ × 15
4 side frames	¾ × ¾ × 31
2 runners	½ × ½ × 20
2 handles	1½ × 1½ × 3

CHILD'S STORAGE CABINET

This storage cabinet (FIG. 6-11) is intended to stand against a wall to gather together early toys and then more complex items as a child grows, followed by books and hobby items. It provides places to keep most of the child's needs as he develops from infant to teenager. There is a broad top to the lower cabinet at a suitable height for a younger child to spread toys and games, then there is a unit for books and many smaller items. Both parts are closed by sliding doors, which hide what might otherwise be regarded as muddles. The sliding doors may be lifted out and could be used as chalkboards or for mounting drawing paper.

The sliding doors and back are thin plywood. All other parts are solid wood, which may be softwood and given a painted finish, or you may prefer polished hardwood to match other furniture in the room. Stiff hardwood might finish 3/4-inch thick, but other wood should finish 7/8-inch thick.

The suggested sizes (FIG. 6-12) are for a unit 48 inches high and 12 inches from front to back. The width is 36 inches, but you may wish to adjust that to suit your

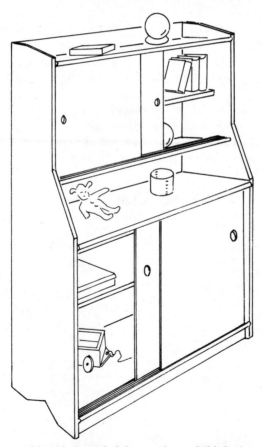

Fig. 6-11. This storage cabinet is intended for use by a child during various stages of his growth.

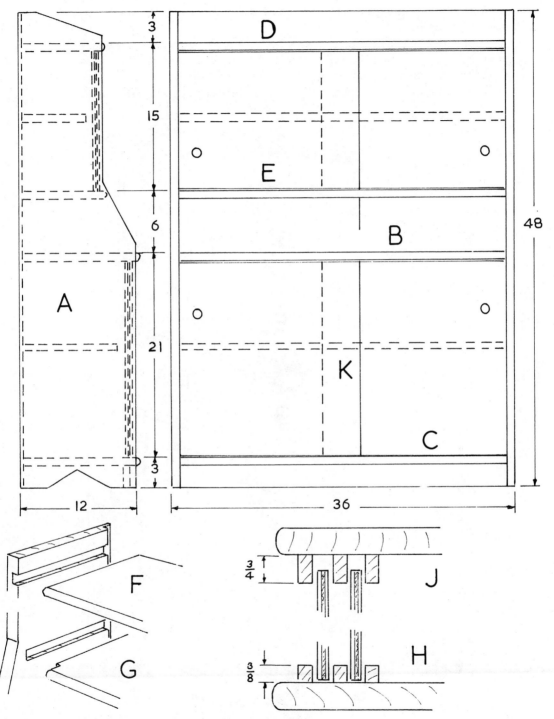

Fig. 6-12. Sizes and details of the child's storage cabinet.

available space. Most joints are dados. Reinforce some of them with screws driven diagonally upwards from below.

Mark out and cut the pair of sides (FIG. 6-12A and 6-13A). Rabbet the rear edges to suit the back plywood. Mark on the positions of the crosswise parts. Shaping is shown cut straight, but you could curve at the changes of section.

Cut the shelves which form the top (FIG. 6-12B and 6-13B) and bottom (FIG. 6-12C

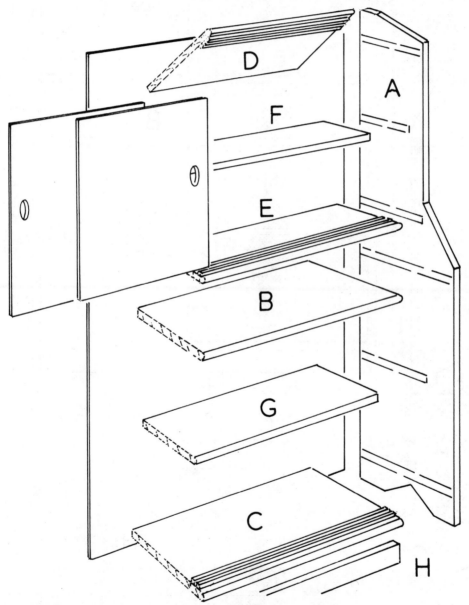

Fig. 6-13. Fitting together parts of the child's storage cabinet.

and 6-13C) of the lower cabinet. They are the same and project forward of the sides with rounded edges.

Prepare the top (FIG. 6-12D and 6-13D) and the bottom (FIG. 6-12E and 6-13E) of the upper cabinet in a similar way.

These shelves determine the width of the cabinet. Cut dados for them in the sides. They go right through the width (FIG. 6-12F), except the one behind the sloping edge (FIG. 6-12G), which is stopped and the shelf notched.

Make the two inside shelves (FIG. 6-13F and G) and cut stopped dados to take them.

Prepare the kickboard (FIG. 6-13H) to go under the bottom shelf. It could be fitted into the sides, but you may find it easier to use dowels into the shelf and the sides.

The sliding doors may be ¼ inch or thicker plywood. The guides are strips glued and pinned to the shelves. Use ¼ inch straight-grained hardwood, even if the rest of the cabinet is softwood. For the bottom guides use strips ⅜-inch high (FIG. 6-12H). For the top guides use strips ¾-inch high (FIG. 6-12J). If the doors are made so they only reach half the depth of the top guides, you will be able to lift the door high enough for its bottom to be pulled clear of the bottom guides. In normal use the doors stay in place by their own weight. Attach the strips with glue and pins, but avoid leaving lumps of glue in the grooves.

Have the back plywood ready. Glue the shelves into their dados and drive screws upwards diagonally from below. Two screws in each main shelf should be enough. Clamp as much as possible and use the back screwed into the rabbets to hold the assembly square.

Make the doors to overlap at the centers by 3 inches or 4 inches (FIG. 6-12K). Drill 1 inch finger holes near the outer edges. Thoroughly sand and lightly round the edges, so they slide smoothly in the grooves. Test the door action and trim edges to fit neatly at the sides.

The doors can be reversed in their grooves. This means you could paint one side of each upper door a matt black or grey, so it can be used as a chalkboard, but it could be turned to the inside when you want the cabinet to present a better appearance when the doors are closed.

Finish softwood with paint or use stain and polish on hardwood.

Materials List for Child's Storage Cabinet

2 sides	⅞ × 12 × 38
2 shelves	⅞ × 9 × 38
1 shelf	⅞ × 1 × 38
1 shelf	⅞ × 7 × 38
1 kickboard	⅞ × 2⅛ × 38
6 guides	¼ × ⅜ × 38
6 guides	¼ × ¾ × 38
1 back	36 × 50 × ¼ or ⅜ plywood
2 doors	20 × 21 × ¼ plywood
2 doors	15 × 20 × ¼ plywood

MULTIPLE STORAGE BIN

There are many situations where storage facilities are needed. If your garden produce has to be kept for a period before it is used in the kitchen, you need some means of storing it together cleanly and safely. In a shop you may have quantities of short ends of wood that could be of use later, together with salvaged hardware and similar things, which should be kept tidy, but accessible. If you have things for sale in a club or store, bins are worth having.

This multiple bin (FIG. 6-14) is designed with garden storage needs in mind, but it could be used for other purposes, either this size or adapted to your needs and available space. Several of these bins may be stacked safely, with the sections still accessible. Two people should have no difficulty in lifting a fully-loaded bin.

You could use any available wood, but sizes (FIG. 6-15) are arranged so most parts can be cut from 1-inch × 12-inch softwood. In its simplest form you could nail all parts of the bin together, but the bin may have to stand up to rough use, and some better ways of joining the ends are suggested.

Check that the sizes suit your needs (FIG. 6-15A). If you alter sizes, make sure the gap at the front is wide enough to admit what you want to store and you can put your hands in easily.

The key parts are the pair of ends (FIG. 6-15B). Cut the two to match.

To resist outward loads from the contents, the lengthwise parts should come between the ends, not on them. You could join them by screwing (FIG. 6-15D)— 10 gauge by 2½-inch screws at 2-inch intervals would be suitable.

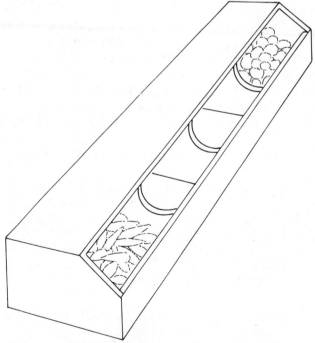

Fig. 6-14. A multiple storage bin may have uses in a kitchen, garage, or garden shed.

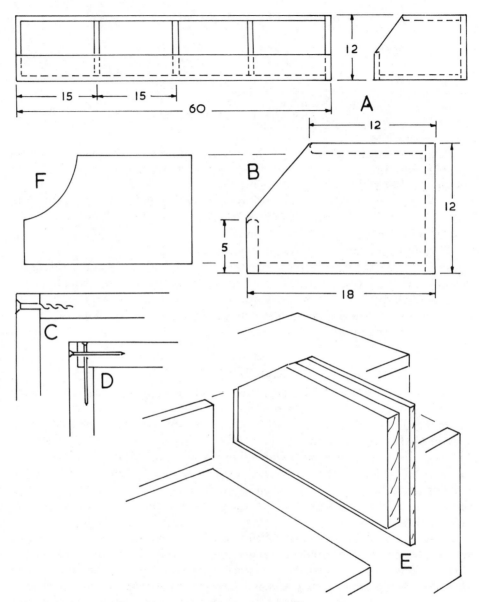

Fig. 6-15. Sizes and construction of the multiple storage bin.

Another method uses nails in both directions, with all the lengthwise parts fitting in rabbets in the ends (FIG. 6-15D and E). Cut the rabbets about two-thirds of the thickness of the ends.

Mark on the ends the thicknesses of the pieces that will be joined, if this is not already shown by rabbets. Use this as a guide to sizes of the three divisions (FIG. 6-15F). Round the edges of the hollows.

Materials List for Multiple Storage Bin

2 ends	1 × 12 × 20
3 divisions	1 × 10 × 18
1 back	1 × 12 × 52
1 top	1 × 11 × 52
1 front	1 × 5 × 52
1 bottom	1 × 16 × 52

Cut the lengthwise pieces. The bottom may have to be two boards, but for most storage purposes you may not consider it necessary to glue them. Round the edges of the boards that come along the opening.

Join the parts together, leaving the top until after you have located and joined the other parts. The divisions could be nailed or screwed in; when everything is assembled there is little risk of them moving.

Except for removing any roughness or projecting edges, there is no need to finish in any special way for most purposes. For food storage you may leave the wood untreated. If you use paint, make sure it is suitable for contact with food. For storage of shop items it may be worthwhile using a light paint inside, so the contents are easy to see. For use elsewhere you may wish to paint a stack of bins to match the surroundings.

KNIFE RACK

Kitchen knives should be kept sharp. This means that their edges need protecting, both to prevent the risk of harming yourself and to prevent them from becoming blunt due to contact with other hard equipment. They could have individual sheaths, which may be practicable if there are only a few; but several knives are better kept in a rack, where they are available for use and their edges are covered. This rack (Fig. 6-16) has knives in two angled lines and is shown suitable for six large knives and seven shorter knives. You could include a sharpening steel or other cook's tool, but the rack should be primarily for knives or other cutting tools.

The suggested design (Fig. 6-17) has a back row suitable for knives with blades up to 8 inches long. The other row takes knives with blades up to 6 inches long. Spacing allows easy gripping of a handle without coming too close to adjoining ones. You could make a rack to suit whatever knives you possess, with slots arranged accordingly, but it would be advisable to allow a few extra slots for knives obtained later. There is no need to make the slots a close fit on each knife blade, so a slot to take the knife with the largest blade section will also suit several smaller ones. Then the cook does not have to find the exact slot when replacing knives.

The rack is best made of hardwood with plywood of the same wood or veneered or stained to match, for the divisions. If the kitchen is equipped with softwood furniture, you could use softwood, but the slots may soon become worn due to contact with the knife edges.

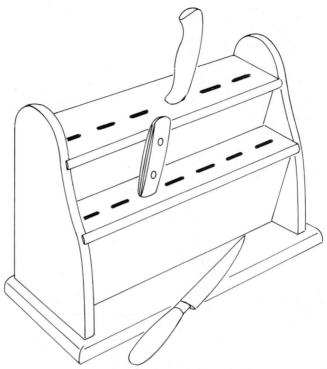

Fig. 6-16. *This knife rack will accommodate knives of several sizes and protect their blades.*

The suggested method of construction is with dado grooves in the ends. These are easily cut with a suitable router cutter, but it would be possible to join the two shelves to the ends with dowels instead of cutting grooves. The plywood divisions would then merely butt against the ends, but the back should be fitted into rabbets.

Mark out the pair of ends (FIG. 6-17A). The drawing shows the layout and angles, but if you wish to set your equipment to the angles, the shelves are at 80° to the rear edge and the divisions are at 90° to them. It should be satisfactory to take all cuts to half the thickness of the ⅝ inch wood.

Cut the grooves and the rabbeted rear edges (FIG. 6-18A). Check that the grooves and rabbets match the finished thicknesses of the other parts.

Prepare the wood for the two shelves, slightly too wide at first. Groove underneath to take the plywood divisions and round the front edges (FIG. 6-17B).

Mark out the knife divisions to suit your knives. The holes should be wide enough for the largest blade in each group, but do not allow excessive clearance, or each knife may be prone to wobble when inserted.

You will probably find the best way to make the slots is to drill at the ends and saw or chisel the waste between, if you do not have a suitable thin router cutter. Smooth each hole with a fine file, if necessary.

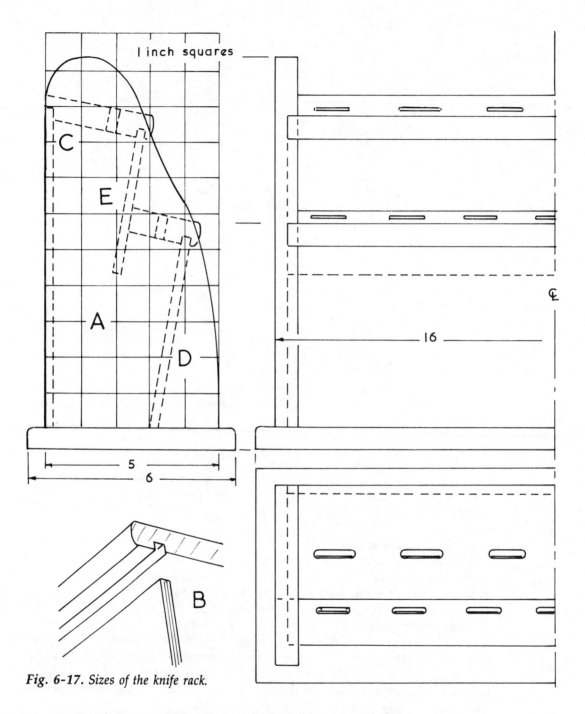

Fig. 6-17. *Sizes of the knife rack.*

Cut the shelves to width. The bottom shelf has a square edge, but the upper one suits the angle of the back and needs a rabbet for the plywood back piece (FIGS. 6-17C and 6-18B).

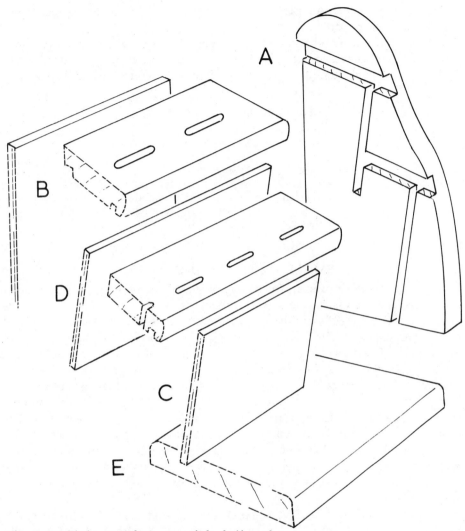

Fig. 6-18. Fitting together parts of the knife rack.

Cut the front division (FIG. 6-17D and 6-18C) to fit into the shelf and ends and reach the bottom edges of the ends.

The other division (FIG. 6-17E and 6-18D) need only project a short distance below the lower shelf.

Glue the plywood into the slotted shelves and all pieces into the end slots. Glue alone should be sufficient, but you could drive a few pins and set them below the surface to cover with stopping.

Fit the back into its rabbets with glue and a few pins. This will strengthen the whole assembly and hold it square.

Make the bottom (FIG. 6-18E) to extend ½ inch all around. Bevel or round its upper edges. Fit it with screws upwards into the ends. If you omit glue in these joints, you will be able to unscrew and retrieve coins if your child decides to use the slots as a piggy bank!

A clear finish will probably be best, but you may need to stain first if you have to match the plywood to the solid wood or you want to match other kitchen equipment. Cloth glued under the bottom will prevent scratching and limit sliding.

Materials List for Knife Rack

2 ends	$\frac{5}{8} \times 5 \times 11$
1 shelf	$\frac{5}{8} \times 4 \times 16$
1 shelf	$\frac{5}{8} \times 3 \times 16$
1 division	$\frac{1}{4} \times 6 \times 16$ plywood
1 division	$\frac{1}{4} \times 5 \times 16$ plywood
1 back	$\frac{1}{4} \times 10 \times 16$ plywood
1 bottom	$\frac{5}{8} \times 6 \times 18$

SMALL CHEST OF DRAWERS

Drawers are the most convenient way of storing many things. They are tidier than boxes and shelves, and share with cupboards the ability to hide what may be unattractive or inherently untidy. Drawers are the best place to keep a variety of small items, paper, or fabric. This small block of drawers (FIG. 6-19) has capacity for many things. The drawer sizes will take papers and books, but are not big enough for bulkier fabric items. The overall size is compact enough to stand in many situations. The height is about the same as a side table and the chest could have many uses. The suggested construction uses plywood for the larger parts, and the sides are given a panelled appearance with solid wood strips on the surface. The carcass is raised off the floor with a narrow kickboard or plinth. Drawer depths taper from the top; this looks better than having them all the same depth, which gives the illusion of depths tapering the other way. If you alter sizes, it is advisable to retain tapered depth sizes. Check that the sizes suggested suit your needs (FIGS. 6-20).

Cut the two sides to size (FIG. 6-20A). At the rear edge the back of the chest will overlap the plywood sides (FIGS. 6-20B and 6-21A). At the front allow for a solid wood covering strip (FIG. 6-21B).

Frame the outside with strips (FIG. 6-21C) to give the panelled effect. Allow the rear strips to overhang enough to cover the back. You could use halving joints on the framing strips, but it should be sufficient to merely butt the corners. Use glue and screws from inside. Put the covering strips on the front edges.

On the inner surfaces of the sides there will be top and bottom frames, then there are runners for the drawers. Mark these positions and attach the runner strips (FIG. 6-21D) with glue and screws from inside. Remove any excess glue, so the drawers will slide smoothly.

The frames (FIG. 6-21E) at top and bottom control the width of the chest. Make them with the shorter strips overlapping the others (for better appearance at the

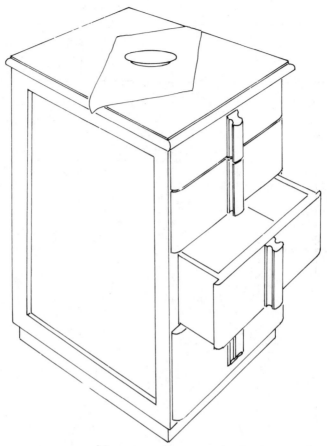

Fig. 6-19. This small chest of drawers may be used beside a bed, in an office or shop, or anywhere that small items have to be stored tidily.

front) and with ¼-inch doweled joints (FIG. 6-20C). Frames come level with the sides at the front and fit inside the back panel.

For attaching the frames to the sides, counterbore the sides of the frame so sunk screws can be driven outwards, at about 6 inch intervals.

Join the top and bottom frames to the sides with glue and screws, then add the back, screwed to the frames and the plywood sides. The back should hold the assembly square, but check that the front is square. If not, put a temporary strip across to hold it in shape while the glue sets.

Make the plinth (FIG. 6-20D) like an open box. It may be level at the back, but at the sides and front, set it in far enough for screws to hold it by being driven downwards through the bottom frame. At the rear corners let the sides overlap the back (FIG. 6-20E). Miter the front corners (FIG. 6-20F). Reinforce the corners with blocks glued inside. Attach the plinth with glue and screws at about 6-inch intervals.

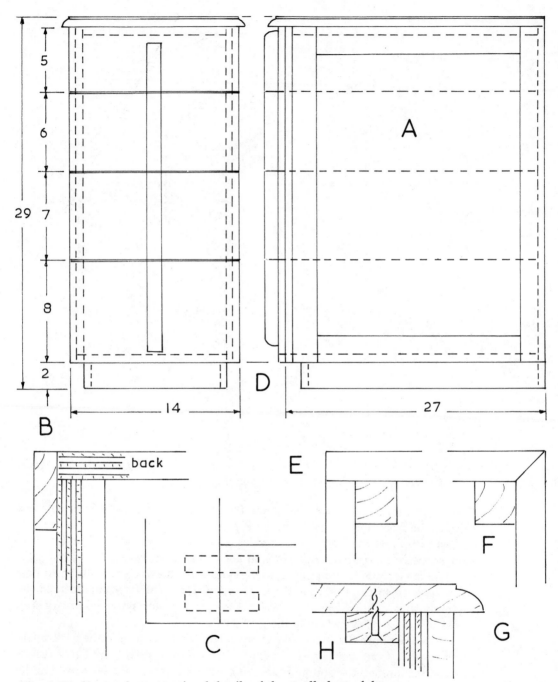

Fig. 6-20. Sizes and constructional details of the small chest of drawers.

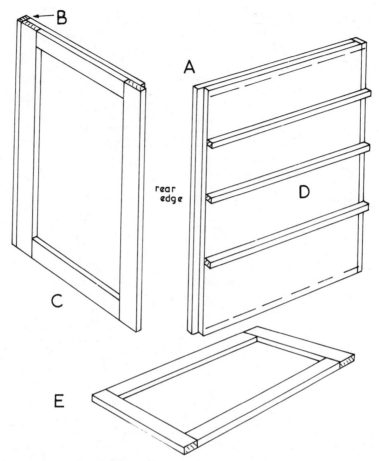

Fig. 6-21. Parts of the carcass of the small chest of drawers.

Do not make and fit the top until after the drawers have been made and fitted, so you can reach inside if it becomes necessary to check the action of drawers as they are fitted.

There are several possible ways of making the drawers. You could make them in the traditional way, with solid wood parts and dovetailed corners. The suggested method of construction (FIG. 6-22) is with ½-inch plywood for the main parts, thin plywood or hardboard for the bottoms, and solid wood fronts. You could use knobs or bought handles; but in this comparatively tall and narrow chest of drawers, vertical handles which close into a single line will look attractive, particularly if the handles are finished a different color from the rest of the fronts.

Each drawer is a box (FIG. 6-22A) with a false front (FIG. 6-22B). The bottom rests on strips inside the box and passes under the drawer back (FIG. 6-22C), to which it is screwed. Use the carcass as a guide to all sizes. The drawers will be stopped by their false fronts when pushed in, so make the drawers to come within no more

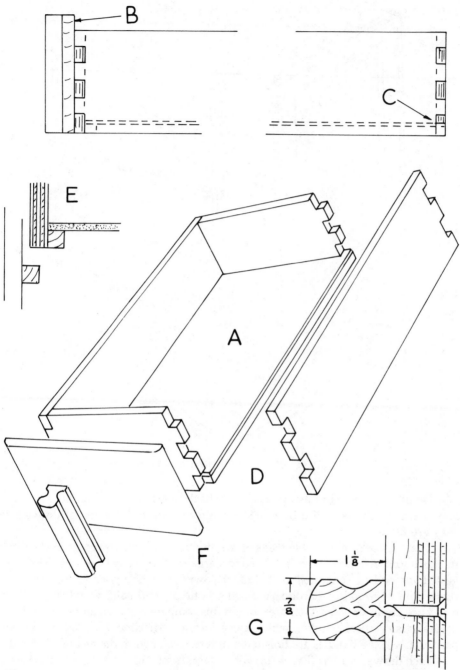

Fig. 6-22. Drawer details for the small chest of drawers.

than ¼ inch of the back, so the drawer cannot touch at the back before the front has met its front surround.

It is advisable to start making drawers from the bottom one up. You can reach and look inside to check fit and action. Cut the sides to fit between the runners. They must slide easily, but avoid excessive slackness. Cut the inner front to the same depth and to fit easily in the width of the opening.

Mark and cut finger joints between these parts (FIG. 6-22D). Finger depths about 1 inch should be satisfactory. Mark for the ½-inch strips and the thickness of the bottom on the sides (FIG. 6-22E). Make the back to come above the bottom and cut its finger joints to the sides. Check sizes in the carcass space.

Glue and nail or screw the bottom bearer strips among the sides and front.

Join the four parts. Use glue and a fine nail or screw through each finger. Slide in the bottom from the back temporarily to hold the assembly square.

When the glue has set, remove any excess and level any projecting parts. Try the drawer in position and make any necessary adjustments. Glue in the bottom with a few pins into the supporting strips. Screw upwards into the back. Make the other three drawers in the same way.

The outer fronts (FIG. 6-22F) have their grain across and should be cut to either reach the outside of the carcass or stop up to ⅛ inch in from its edges. The top three drawer outer fronts have their lower edges level with the bottoms of the drawers. The top drawer outer front overlaps the edge of the top frame. The next two drawer fronts overlap the ends of the runners above. The bottom outer front overlaps the runners above and may be cut level at the bottom or allowed to overlap the edge of the frame.

Round the ends of the fronts. Join them to their inner fronts with glue and screws from inside. Four screws near the corners should be enough.

Make the handles in one length, to the suggested section (FIG. 6-22G). Mark the positions on the drawers and drill for two screws from inside in each front.

Cut the handles to come level with the tops and bottoms of the intermediate drawers, but let the top and bottom handles stop short of the edges, then round or bevel them. Fit the handles with glue and screws.

Check the fit and action of the drawers before you make and fit the chest top. Candle wax rubbed on drawer edges will help them run smoothly.

The top may be made of solid wood, probably with pieces glued to make up the width. You could use plywood edged with solid wood. You could make the top to finish level all around, but it is suggested with an overhang at front and sides (FIG. 6-20G). Arrange the overhang above the closed drawer front to be the same as you allow at the sides. Round or mold the outer edges.

Attach the top with screws upwards through the top frame (FIG. 6-20H). You could use glue as well, but if you depend on screws only to allow a little movement, slight expansion and contraction of the wood should not cause cracking; and if you ever need to get at the inside of the chest, you can remove the top.

It is usual to leave the insides of drawers and the surrounding carcass untreated, but you can finish the outsides to match other furniture. Darkening the handles provides an interesting contrast. You may prefer to stain them before assembly.

Materials List for Small Chest of Drawers

½-inch plywood

2 sides	26½ × 27
1 back	13 × 27
2 drawer sides	7½ × 27
2 drawer sides	7 × 27
2 drawer sides	6 × 27
2 drawer sides	5 × 27
1 drawer front	7½ × 14
1 drawer front	7 × 14
1 drawer front	6 × 14
1 drawer front	6 × 14
1 drawer back	5 × 14
1 drawer back	7 × 14
1 drawer back	6½ × 14
1 drawer back	5½ × 14
1 drawer back	4½ × 14

Solid wood

4 side frames	½ × 2 × 27
4 side frames	½ × 2 × 24
4 inside frames	⅝ × 1½ × 14
4 inside frames	⅝ × 1½ × 25
6 drawer runners	½ × ½ × 28
8 drawer bottoms	½ × ½ × 28
4 drawer bottoms	½ × ½ × 14
2 plinths	½ × 2 × 27
2 plinths	½ × 2 × 14
1 drawer front	½ × 8 × 16
1 drawer front	½ × 7 × 16
1 drawer front	½ × 6 × 16
1 drawer front	½ × 5 × 16
handles from	⅞ × 1⅛ × 29
1 top	⅝ × 16 × 29

Hardboard

4 drawer bottoms	14 × 27

SEWING BOX

To hold all the equipment and work of an enthusiastic needlewoman or knitter, there has to be a container of good capacity with parts that will keep the many small items tidy, but accessible. This box on supporting stands forms an attractive piece of furniture, without its main use being obvious (FIG. 6-23). Its height is less than that of a table and should be suitable for the user to reach from a chair. The box has a lift-out tray for small items and the lid is also removable. It

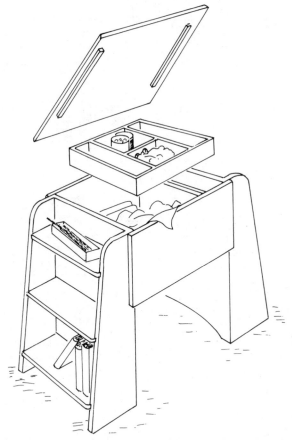

Fig. 6-23. *This sewing box has a tray and lift-off lid and is supported by bookcase ends.*

could be hinged, but lifting away completely gives maximum access to the interior. The supports are made like bookcases. Although they would hold books, patterns, and similar things, they could be used for ornaments, small plants or other decorative features.

Sizes (FIG. 6-24) are not critical and you could make a sewing box of different sizes to suit needs or available space in the same way. The instructions apply to solid wood construction, with a little plywood, but it would be possible to use veneered particleboard throughout, with iron-on edging where needed. Instead of dado joints for the shelves, there would have to be dowels and the top corners of the supports should be cut square, as iron-on edging does not bond securely on close curves.

The main parts are assumed to be hardwood, probably matching existing furniture. Softwood is not advised, but if you want to match 'knotty pine' or similar furniture, it could be used.

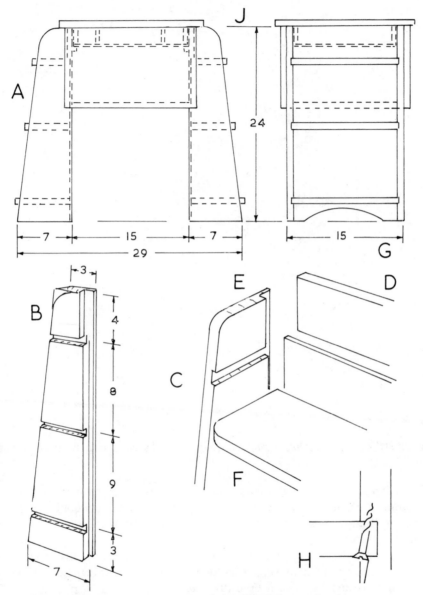

Fig. 6-24. Sizes and some constructional details of the sewing box.

The two supports are the same and made first as complete units. The box is not independent, but it makes use of the backs of the supports, which it joins with overlapping sides and an inserted bottom.

Make the two pairs of support sides (FIG. 6-24A). Cut to the tapers (FIG. 6-24B), but leave rounding the top corners until other work has been done on the wood.

Cut rabbets to suit the plywood backs the full lengths of the pieces. Be careful to match them as pairs.

The shelves will project outside the tapered edges, so you can cut the dado joints right through (FIG. 6-24C). See that the widths of the grooves will make a close fit on the shelves.

There will be solid wood backs above the top shelves (FIG. 6-24D). Deepen the rabbets above the shelf groove to allow for this (FIG. 6-24E).

Round the top corners and take sharpness off all exposed edges.

Make the shelves wide enough to project the same amount—³/₄-inch would be suitable. Check that all shelves are exactly the same length. Round the outer corners and edges (FIG. 6-24F).

Make the solid wood backs to match. Cut the plywood backs to fit. Hollow the edges that will meet the floor (FIG. 6-24G). Drill the solid backs ready for screwing in place. The plywood back will be neater if pins to the sides and shelves are used to supplement glue.

Glue the shelves in their grooves and fit the backs to hold the assembly square. Glue alone should be sufficient with closely fitting shelves, but if you think additional security is needed, drive a screw diagonally upwards under the outer edges of the bottom shelves (FIG. 6-24H).

Remove surplus glue and do any necessary trimming or sanding. See that the supports match. It is important that their tops come level when they are standing on a level surface.

The box sides overlap the supports by 1 inch (FIG. 6-25A).

Prepare the sides and supports for ³/₈-inch dowels (FIG. 6-25B). Drill as deeply as possible, without the drill bit breaking through. Four dowels to supplement glue in each joint should be sufficient.

Join the box sides to the supports. Clamp tightly until the glue has set. Have the assembly standing on a level surface and check that the top corners are square.

Put ¹/₂-inch-square strips around the bottom of the box, glued and pinned or screwed in place (FIG. 6-25C). Fit the plywood bottom on these supports.

Put similar strips across the supports (FIG. 6-25D) to hold the tray, which should fit about ¹/₈ inch below the top edge. You may prefer to leave fitting these strips until you have made the tray and are certain of its depth.

The tray may be just a simple box into which the user puts containers and re-arranges things as needed. The alternative is to build in divisions (FIG. 6-26A). The tray should make an easy fit in the box and rest on supporting strips (FIG. 6-26B) at the ends.

The box corners could be simply overlapped and screwed. They could be dovetailed. Finger joints are shown (FIG. 6-26C). They may be glued and pinned both ways to make strong corners. The divisions may be fitted into grooves, although it should be sufficient to glue and pin or screw them.

Mark out and cut the tray parts so there will be a little excess wood projecting through the corner joints, to be leveled after assembly. The divisions may be level with the outsides of the tray or be kept a little lower and their top edges rounded.

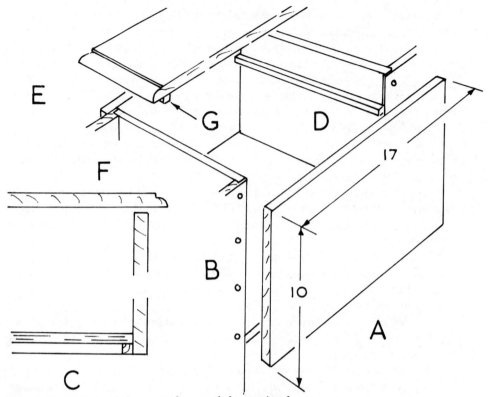

Fig. 6-25. Details of the central part of the sewing box.

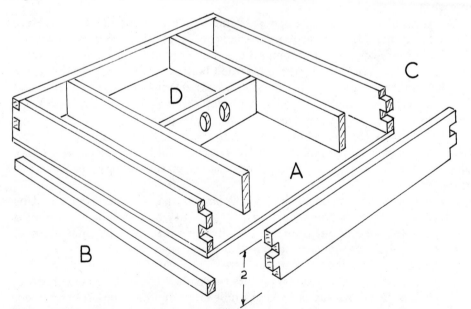

Fig. 6-26. Details of a suggested tray for the sewing box.

Drill two 1 inch holes in the middle division (FIG. 6-26D), so fingers can be used to lift out the tray. Round the hole edges. Glue and pin on the bottom. Trim outside and remove sharp edges.

Make the top (FIGS. 6-24J and 6-25E) to overlap ¾ inch all around. Edges may be left square or be rounded or molded (FIG. 6-25F).

Put strips under the ends of the top (FIG. 6-25G) to drop into the tops of the supports. Allow enough clearance for easy fitting, but the top should not be able to move much when in position.

Finish with stain and polish or as you wish to match other furniture.

Materials List for Sewing Box

4 support sides	¾ × 7 × 26
2 shelves	¾ × 7½ × 16
2 shelves	¾ × 6 × 16
2 shelves	¾ × 4½ × 16
2 backs	¾ × 4 × 16
2 backs	15 × 21 × ¼ plywood
2 box sides	¾ × 10 × 19
1 top	¾ × 19 × 21
1 box bottom	15 × 15 × ½ plywood
6 strips	½ × ½ × 16
7 tray parts	½ × 2 × 16
1 tray bottom	16 × 16 × ¼ plywood

7

Built-in Furniture

If you attach furniture to a wall you can use the structure of the house to provide rigidity, so the table, rack, or other item may be taller or narrower than would be wise if it was freestanding. The wall may also form part of the piece, or in a corner two parts of it, so you'll have to construct less. With built-in furniture, you can maximize use of the space, fill a recess in a way that no independent article could, and in most situations, leave more of the room for use or other furniture.

You cannot move built-in furniture about, so you must be certain you want it exactly where you fit it. Quite often it is going where you would not put another item, in any case. In a restricted place, building in may be the only way of providing the furniture you want.

Check that the walls are suitable for taking screws. Thin panels may not be, but you can usually find studs or other solid supports and arrange the furniture accordingly. Brick or stone will give great support, but will have to be plugged.

It should be safe to assume that floors are level and walls are vertical, but you should not assume that all corners are 90°. A corner may be, but you should check, as described in the first project instructions; otherwise, if you make the furniture square and the corner is not, you will have gaps that could spoil fit and appearance.

CORNER SHELVES

A block of shelves can utilize a corner of any room that might not otherwise be occupied. The size of shelves and how many you fit depends on your needs and available space. The suggested arrangement (FIG. 7-1) has three shelves with supports to the floor, but you could carry the shelves to the ceiling, or you could leave

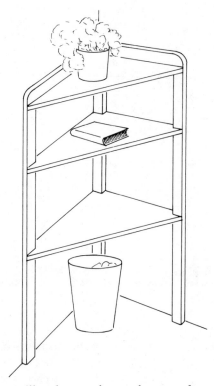

Fig. 7-1. Corner shelves will make use of part of a room that may otherwise be empty.

off the legs if you need space below hanging shelves, as when the shelves are to provide storage above a corner built-in table. Instructions suit the shelves shown, but you can alter sizes and adapt the arrangement to fit your needs.

For these shelves and any other furniture to be fitted into a room corner, you should start by checking the angle of the corner. Put a try square in the corner. If that is found to match, go ahead making the shelves square; but if it does not, plane a piece of scrap plywood or hardboard, extending at least as far as the shelves, so it fits the corner (FIG. 7-2A). Use this instead of a square for marking shelves and any other parts that have to fit into the corner.

Mark out three uprights (FIG. 7-2B) with the positions of the shelves. Notch at each position (FIG. 7-2C) to fit closely on the shelves. Round the top corners of the outer uprights.

Make the three shelves (FIG. 7-2D and E). See that the corner angles match the room walls. Notch to fit the uprights.

For shop or garage you may leave the plywood front edges exposed, but elsewhere the appearance will be improved by gluing and pinning on a solid wood lip (FIG. 7-2F).

Cut strips to fit between the tops and the uprights (FIG. 7-2G). The lower

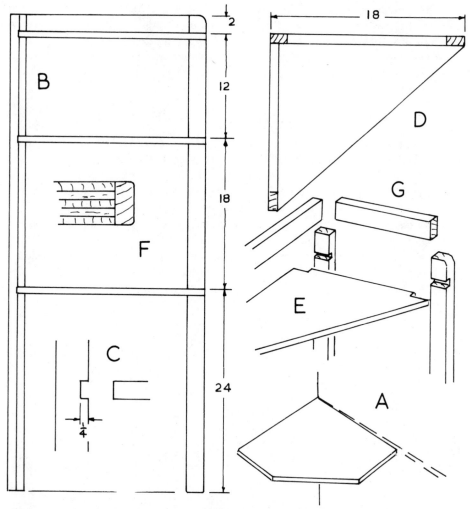

Fig. 7-2. Sizes and constructional details of the corner shelves.

Materials List for Corner Shelves

3 uprights	$1 \times 2 \times 60$
2 tops	$1 \times 2 \times 16$
3 shelves	$18 \times 33 \times \frac{1}{2}$ plywood
3 lips	$\frac{1}{4} \times \frac{1}{2} \times 33$ optional

shelves are shown without strips, but you could fit them if you wish to keep anything on the shelves from touching the walls.

Glue the shelves into their notches in the uprights and screw with heads on the wall sides of the uprights. The top strips could be doweled into the uprights and the shelf, or merely glued and screwed upwards through the shelf.

The legs to the floor will take the weight of the assembly. You may find it sufficient to only drive one screw through each outer upright to hold the shelves to the wall, or it may be necessary to use more to get a close fit.

How you finish the unit depends on its situation and the wood used. It could be painted or given a stain and polish finish to match other furniture.

CORNER CUPBOARD

If you want something more enclosed than shelves built into a corner, you can make a cupboard. This could be combined with open shelves and may have legs to the floor, but the example shown (FIG. 7-3) is a self-contained small cupboard mounted in the corner of a room. To give greater capacity than is possible with a simple triangular section, there are sides extending from each wall.

The backs are plywood and you could use plywood for the top and bottom, with solid wood edging. For use in a living room, the facing wood should be hardwood, but elsewhere you may use softwood, which is finished with paint.

To obtain the exact sections of some parts, it is necessary to set out a full-size

Fig. 7-3. A corner cupboard may be hung at a convenient height in a position that might not otherwise be used.

view from above. This is most easily done if you cut the wood for a top or bottom first. See that the corner angle matches that of the room, as detailed in the previous project. There is no need to finish the outer parts to size yet.

Mark out the positions of the upright parts (FIG. 7-4A). Allow for the edge to extend ⅜ inch when finished. The plywood backs fit into rabbets (FIG. 7-4B) and the front pieces have to be mitered together (FIG. 7-4C).

With the setting out as a guide, prepare the wood for the sides (FIG. 7-5A). Cut rabbets to suit the plywood and bevel the other edges.

Make the front strips (FIG. 7-5B). Bevel to match the other pieces and see that you keep the wood parallel, so the door will fit properly.

Make the top crossbar (FIG. 7-5C). It could be doweled between the uprights, but there is not much space for drilling and it would be better to cut stub tenons (FIG. 7-4D).

Glue the beveled uprights. Plain glued joints should be satisfactory, but if you think extra strength is advisable, you could use a few dowels, or plates if you have suitable equipment.

Cut the plywood backs (FIG. 7-5D). Allow for one overlapping the other, to be joined with a few screws. Drill for screws into the front rabbets.

Complete the cutting of top and bottom to size and drill for screws into the other parts. Round the exposed edges.

Join the plywood parts to each other. Fit the top crossbar between the uprights and glue and screw the plywood backs to the rabbets. Check the assembly against the top and bottom.

Cut the shelf to size (FIG. 7-5E). It is shown as a triangle, so it does not project forward as far as the door. Position it just above the center of the cabinet. You could screw through the backs or put cleats on them for the shelf to rest on.

Join the top and bottom to the other parts. See that the door opening remains parallel. It should be satisfactory to use countersunk screws, but if you want to hide their heads, the holes might be counterbored and plugged.

The door is a plain board (FIG. 7-5F). Cut it with sufficient clearance to fit easily. Use two 2-inch hinges at one side. There may be a spring or magnetic catch and stop at the other side. You could use a bought knob or handle, but a shaped strip of wood 5 inches long is suggested (FIG. 7-4E).

Materials List for Corner Cupboard

1 top	⅝ × 11 × 18
1 bottom	⅝ × 11 × 18
2 backs	12 × 19 × ½ plywood
2 sides	¾ × 3 × 19
2 fronts	¾ × 2 × 19
1 crossbar	¾ × 1 × 11
1 shelf	⅝ × 9 × 17
1 door	¾ × 9 × 18
1 handle	¾ × 1 × 6

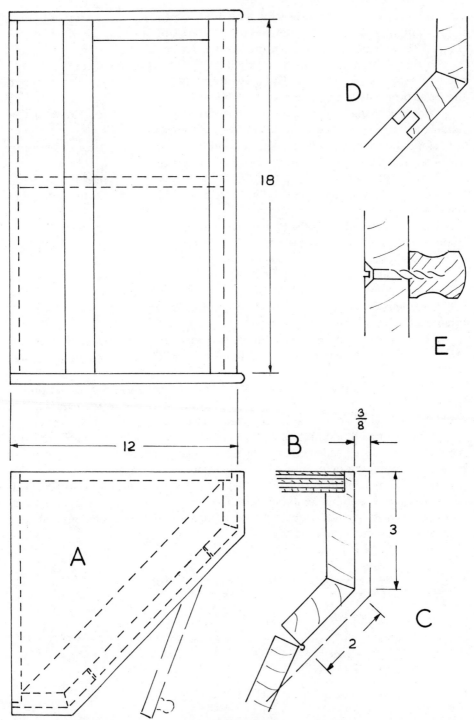

Fig. 7-4. Sizes and sections of the corner cupboard.

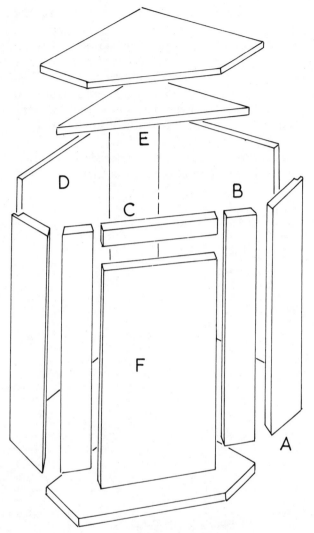

Fig. 7-5. How the parts of the corner cupboard fit together.

Attach the cupboard to the walls with screws through the backs.

Apply paint or stain and polish. Giving the inside a lighter treatment makes the contents more easily seen.

CORNER TABLE

Walls can provide rigidity to a table or bench. They can also provide support so less structure is needed. If you can build the table into a corner, only one leg will be needed (FIG. 7-6A). A similar table could be used away from a corner, but then two legs would be required. In both cases the table takes up less space than a freestanding table and it cannot be accidentally moved or knocked over. The example is a small table for general use, or it could form a desk or a bench for a hobby. There is clearance for your legs when sitting on a normal chair.

The table would look best in hardwood and finished with stain and polish, but softwood could be painted. For some purposes a plywood top may be adequate alone or covered with laminated plastic, for kitchen or utility room use. In a living room the top might be solid wood with molded edges.

The leg and top frame are made first, then attached to the wall (FIG. 7-6B) and the top added last. Make the leg and fit other parts to it.

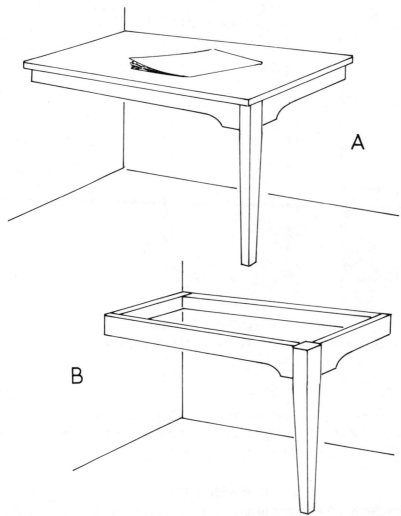

Fig. 7-6. A table fitted into a corner uses the walls for support and only needs one leg.

The leg is 2½ inches square to 6 inches from the top, then it tapers to 1½ inches square at the floor. Mark it out, but leave planing the tapers until you have done the drilling for dowels, so it is easier to keep the wood level while drilling.

Mark out the front rail (FIG. 7-7A) and end rail (FIG. 7-7B). The curves between the different widths look better as sweeping shapes like parts of ellipses than as parts of circles.

Mark out and drill for ½-inch dowels (FIG. 7-7C). Drill until the holes meet in the leg, to get maximum glue area.

Taper the leg and cut the rails to shape. Take sharpness off the lower edges.

Make the two wall rails (FIG. 7-7D). Check that sizes will assemble to a true shape, but if the room corner is out of square allow for it. Drill these rails for dowel joints to each other and the outer rails (FIG. 7-7E).

Drill the rear rails for screws to the walls—three in the long rail and two in the short one should be enough.

Drill all four rails for pocket screws upwards into the top (FIG. 7-7F). Space these at about 6 inch intervals along the insides of the outer rails, but they can be further apart in the wall rails.

Join the parts together. Check that there is no twist in the top by sighting across or assembling inverted on a flat surface.

Attach the assembly to the wall. The leg will settle height, but measure to check that the wall rails are parallel to the floor. Mark through the screw holes and prepare the wall for screwing, then drive them.

Start preparing the top by planing the rear edges to fit closely to the walls. The other edges should be parallel to the framing. The top is shown overhanging the leg by 2 inches, which should suit most purposes, but if you will want to clamp on tools or kitchen appliances, allow sufficient overlap.

Finish the outer edges to suit the purpose. You may leave it square for a bench. If the top is covered with laminated plastic you could use metal or plastic edging. A solid wood top could be left square or molded. Keep any molding narrow (FIG. 7-7G). If you round the edge, an elliptical section (FIG. 7-7H) looks better than a semicircle. The projecting top corner could be rounded.

Attach the top by screwing upwards. Deal with the wall rails first, to get the edges of the top tight against the walls, then screw from the outer rails.

You could apply a finish after complete assembly, but it may be better to paint or stain and polish the top before screwing it in place. This gives you easier access for finishing the underframing.

Materials List for Corner Table

1 leg	2½ × 2½ × 31
1 rail	1 × 5 × 33
1 rail	1 × 5 × 15
1 rail	1 × 2 × 33
1 rail	1 × 2 × 15
1 top	¾ × 18 × 38

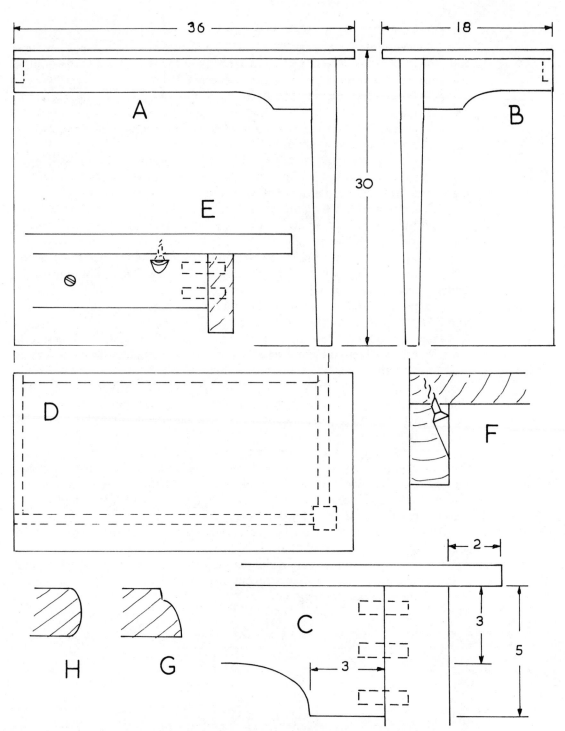

Fig. 7-7. Sizes and constructional methods of the corner table.

RECESS STORAGE

If there is a recess in a room, it is easy to convert it to a closet or other storage. You can fit in a tabletop, similar to the one just described, but without even the need for one leg. You could fit a top and add doors below. You can put up shelves to make a bookcase. One of the simplest ways to convert the recess is to fit a top and hang curtains below, instead of doors, to hide the contents. If you arrange this high and fit a rail across, you have a clothes closet. If the top is at table height, you will have a working or storage surface and plenty of storage below (Fig. 7-8).

It would be possible to extend the top from the recess, but that would entail fitting a side. In a recess of reasonable depth it is usually better to set the top back a few inches (Fig. 7-9A).

The only significant difficulty is in getting a close fit. Because of the two corners involved, you cannot make a trial assembly, then true edges to fit. Your first assembly is the final one. Put lines on the walls at the height you want to fit the top. Try a square in the two corners at this level. If these show accurate corners, you have no problem. Measure across at the rear and front of the recess. If these are the same, you have no problem. If there are noticeable differences in angles or measurements, you have to allow for them.

If you have to allow for inaccuracies, make the top first or use a piece of hardboard or scrap plywood to use as a template after checking it fits. Mark on its rear edge the width of the recess. Measure on the walls equal distances from the corners each way at top level (Fig. 7-9B). Repeat the measurements on the top or the template at the width marks. Measure distances between the points on the wall

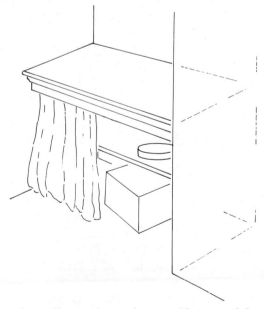

Fig. 7-8. In a recess the walls may be used to provide most of the support for storage arrangements.

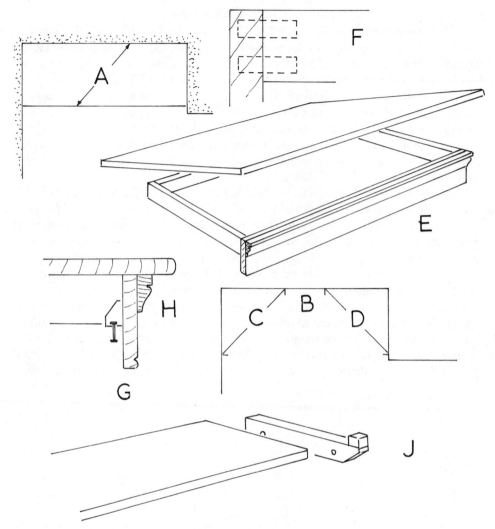

Fig. 7-9. Parts for the top and shelf in recess storage.

(FIG. 7-9C and D). Repeat these on the top or its template. Draw lines through these points to show the end cuts of the top. Mark the width of the top. Check the width you have marked on the top with the matching width across the recess.

Cut the ends of the top and test the piece in the recess. Leave cutting the front edge of the top until you have made and fitted the rails. Use it as a guide to lengths of other parts.

The underframing consists of three strips attached to the wall and a deeper piece at the front to take a curtain rail. That may be decorated with an applied molding (FIG. 7-9E). Plan this layout to suit the recess at the marked level.

Materials List for Recess Storage

(Sizes depend on the recess, but these are suggested sections)

1 top	³⁄₄ thick
1 front rail	³⁄₄ × 4
1 back rail	1 × 2
2 side rails	1 × 2
1 shelf	³⁄₄ thick
2 cleats	³⁄₄ × 1¹⁄₂

Obtain the curtain rail and its attachments. For a wide recess you may prefer two rails overlapping at the center. Check what depth will be needed for the curtains to hang and slide so they are adequately covered at the top. A front board 4 inches deep should be enough.

Prepare the strips on the wall. There is no need for dowels or other joints where they meet each other, but allow for the side strips being doweled to the front piece (FIG. 7-9F).

Make the front board. The bottom edge could be beveled or rounded, or you may prefer to work a bead on it (FIG. 7-9G).

Drill all strips for pocket screws upwards into the top, as described for the corner table (FIG. 7-7F) — a 6-inch spacing along the front and twice that around the edges should be sufficient, as any upward loads on the top may be expected to be only slight. Position the pocket screws in the front rail so you will be able to drive them after the curtain rail brackets have been screwed on.

A strip molding along the front (FIG. 7-9H) is not essential, but it improves appearance.

Screw the strips to the wall, and glue and dowel the front to the end ones.

If you want to fit a shelf, do this before adding the top. It could be fixed permanently, but it is more convenient to be able to lift out. Do not make the shelf too wide or it may interfere with access to the space below — not much more than half the width of the top will be about right.

Screw supporting cleats to the walls (FIG. 7-9J). Blocks at the front prevent the shelf sliding forward, but it can be lifted out.

Screw the curtain rail in place, and you may wish to test the action of the curtains before screwing on the top.

Try the top in position. Mark the overhang of the front parallel with the supporting strip. Its edge could be molded, but if there is a strip of molding below, it should be sufficient to lightly round it.

Finish will depend on the situation and nearby furniture. After a trial assembly it will be best to finish the top before it is finally screwed in position.

FOLDING DESK

Office facilities, possibly of a very limited sort, are needed in most homes, if only to deal with bills and correspondence. A desk as a piece of independent furniture may not be justified. This folding desk (FIG. 7-10) is intended to be attached to a wall, from which it projects less than 12 inches. When opened there is a flat working surface projecting a further 24 inches and about 10 inches of internal surfaces and shelving for use. Underneath there is plenty of shelving for storage of books or stationery. The doors that enclose the lower part act as supports for the working surface. The flap swings upwards and hides the contents of the upper part, so it is not obvious that the unit is a desk. Length and the swing of doors are related, and the desk, as shown, is just over 36 inches long (FIG. 7-11). Main parts of the unit are solid wood, but the flap and two doors could be ¾ inch plywood edged with solid wood, or you could use veneered particleboard. For a

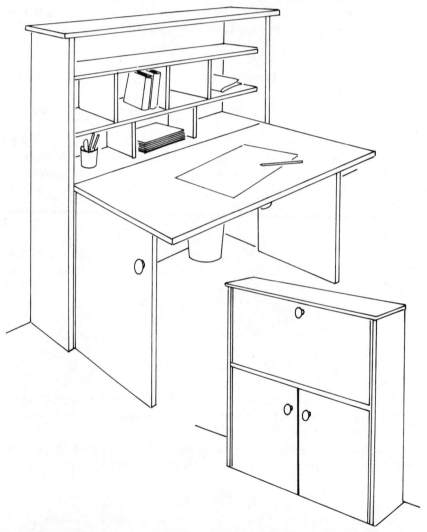

Fig. 7-10. This folding desk or hobby bench can be folded flat so its contents are hidden.

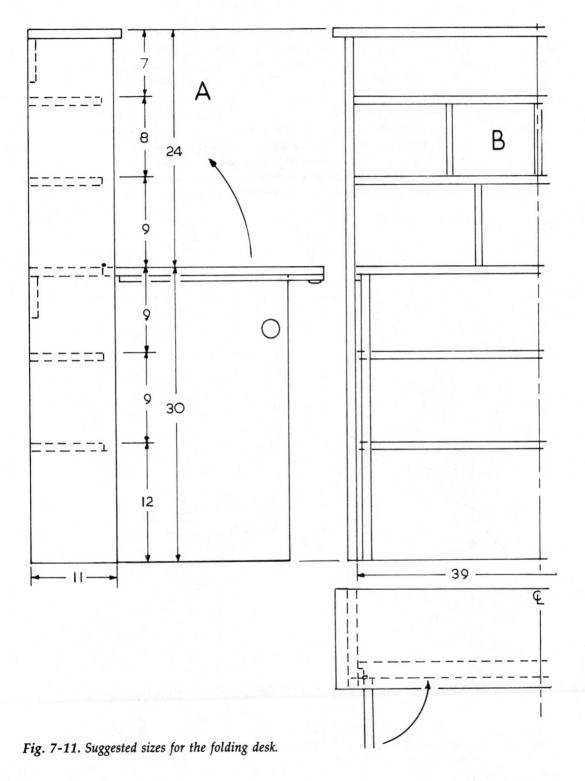

Fig. 7-11. Suggested sizes for the folding desk.

piece of furniture to match other furniture, use hardwood and have veneered pieces for the plywood parts. For a painted finish, which might be suitable for a child's room, or a shop or basement where the desk will serve more as a hobby bench, you could use softwood and finish it with paint. Internal parts might be softwood in any case.

It would be possible to use dado joints for most parts, but doweling is suggested. Use four ½-inch dowels in the wide parts (FIG. 7-13A) and two in each of the rear strips (FIG. 7-12A and B and 7-13B). Drill holes as deep as possible in the sides, without the drill breaking through, to get maximum glue area.

Mark out the pair of sides (FIG. 7-11A and 7-12D) with the positions of the other parts. The shelves behind the flap and in the top section are kept back from the

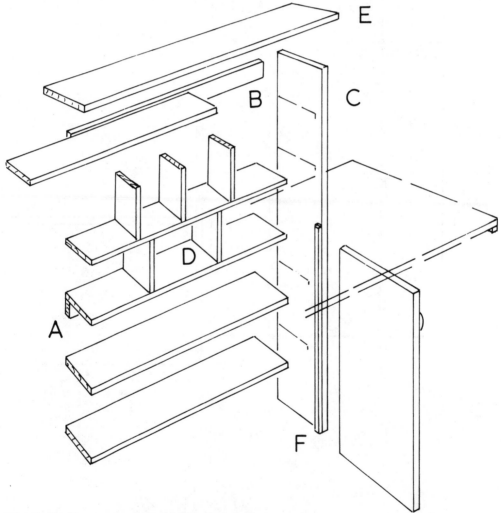

Fig. 7-12. How parts of the folding desk are put together.

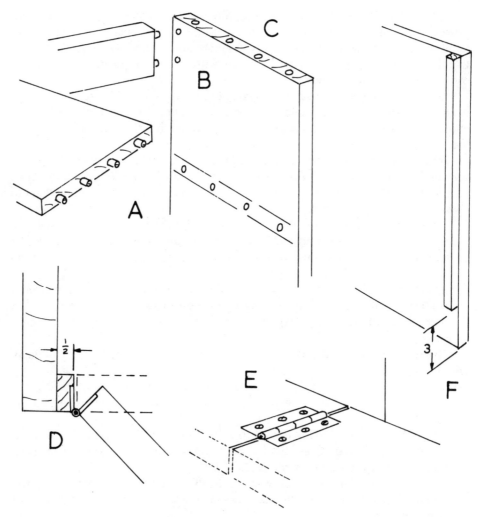

Fig. 7-13. Joints for parts of the folding desk.

front edge by the thickness of the flap and its edge strips, with ⅛ inch for clearance. The bottom shelves are kept back from the front edge by the thickness of the doors, for which they act as stops.

Make the shelves and the two strips for attaching to the wall all the same length. Prepare the ends and the uprights for the dowel joints.

You will probably settle for plain shelves in the lower part, but in the upper section there could be divisions. One arrangement is suggested (FIG. 7-11B and 7-12D). Arrange compartments to suit your needs, but the width of shelves should suit standard typing paper laid flat, so space at least some of the uprights to allow for this. Round the front edges of the divisions. Prepare them for dowels, which may be ⅜-inch diameter if you are using thinner wood. Take sharpness off the front edges of the shelves.

Check the depths of all dowel holes and see they are clear. Have sufficient dowels ready and assemble all parts made so far in one operation. See that all joints are pulled tight and the assembly is square and without twist. It will be best to glue with the back down on a flat surface, with weights applied, if necessary, to control any tendency to twist.

Make the top (FIG. 7-12E) to come level at the back, but overhang about 1 inch at front and ends. Round or mold the overhanging parts. Prepare for dowels at the ends (FIG. 7-13C). Arrange a few dowels widely spaced into the rear rail. Join on the top.

Put strips inside the fronts of the uprights to come as high as the underside of the shelf behind the flap. These are ½-inch wide and as thick as the doors (FIG. 7-12F and 7-13D) to keep the doors far enough in from the uprights to allow them to open against stops on the flap.

The flap or working top has to fit neatly between the uprights, without excessive clearance. It fits under the overhanging top when closed and its lower edge then should be level with the top of its shelf. This allows it to swing down so both of these surfaces are level.

Make the flap from plywood with solid wood edging or from veneered particleboard with wood or iron-on edging to these sizes.

Let in four hinges (FIG. 7-13E) with knuckles upwards. Brass hinges 2 inches long would be neat.

Try the action of the flap with a few temporary screws in the hinges, but delay final fitting until later.

Attach ½ inch square strips to the outside edges of the flap to act as stops when the flap is lowered to the working position and the doors swung out as supports (FIG. 7-13F).

Make the doors for the lower part to match the flap. Top edges should reach the lowered flap. Lower edges should almost reach the floor. Arrange widths so the doors meet at the center of the desk.

Put two hinges on each door attached to the strips on the uprights. Let the hinges in sufficiently so when the doors are swung out they will come inside the stops on the flap.

Arrange spring or magnetic catches behind the doors on one of the shelves. If you want more positive fastening, use a bolt on the inside of one door to attach it to a shelf, then a fastener on the other door to hold it to the first.

Materials List for Folding Desk

2 sides	1 × 11 × 56
1 top	1 × 12 × 44
5 shelves	¾ × 10 × 40
3 divisions	⅝ × 10 × 9
2 divisions	⅝ × 10 × 10
2 packings	½ × ¾ × 32
2 edge strips	½ × ½ × 22
1 flap	¾ × 23 × 40
2 doors	¾ × 20 × 32

Two ball catches in the top edge of the flap should be sufficient to hold it to the overhanging top.

A handle or knob at the center of the top of the flap may be used to pull it down. Arrange handles at comfortable heights on the doors.

It will probably be sufficient to have two screws through each rear strip into the wall. Position them to go into studs. If there is a baseboard around the room, cut the uprights to clear it.

Finish the wood to suit the situation. You may leave the internal surfaces untreated or just seal their grain with varnish. The working surface is best without a gloss.

FOLD-DOWN TABLE

When space is limited and you need a table occasionally, a normal table may be a nuisance when it is not required. This may happen in a small hall or even in a large room where a side table is important on occasions, but would be better out of the way at other times. A table attached to the wall in the form of a flap that swings down will be as good as a freestanding table when erected, but it swings down against the wall to project only a few inches.

This table (FIG. 7-14A and B) has a narrow part attached to the wall, then the tabletop is hinged to it and can be held up by a gateleg or a bracket. When folded down, the thickness is 4 inches. As drawn (FIG. 7-15), the table ready for use is 21 inches wide and 36 inches long. You could make the table in other sizes to suit your needs in the same way.

The table will look attractive if made completely of solid wood, but you may prefer to use plywood with solid wood edging or veneered particleboard for the top, to avoid the need to glue several boards together. If you glue boards, you can reduce the risk of warping if end grain markings are through the thickness of the wood, or if you cannot obtain boards cut this way, with grain of alternate boards opposite ways.

Two types of support are suggested. The first has a gateleg going to the floor (FIG. 7-14C and 7-15A). That is the strongest form, but if you would prefer not to have the leg, as in a very restricted space or where maximum knee room for sitters is needed, there can be a bracket (FIG. 7-14D and 7-17A).

The suggested height is 28 inches from the floor. If the wall is without a baseboard, the upright can go to the floor. If there is a baseboard, cut it off above it. Attachment to the wall has to be secure. On a hollow wall with studs, locate the upright so screws can go through into a stud. Screws through the horizontal part will also have to be spaced to suit studs. This may affect positioning of the table, although altering the location of the upright in relation to the top can be by a few inches, if that gives a better attachment.

The wall assembly (FIG. 7-14E and F and 7-16A) may be joined together with ½-inch dowels at about 12-inch intervals.

Make the upright (FIG. 7-14G) to fit squarely in position. It could be doweled to the horizontal strip, but is shown lapped into the back (FIG. 7-16B).

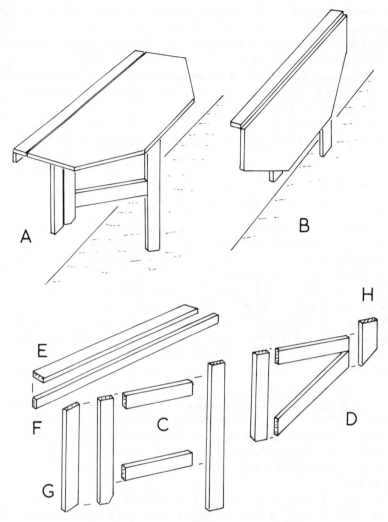

Fig. 7-14. *A table supported on the wall may fold down to occupy minimum space. This table may be made with a swinging gate leg or a bracket.*

If you choose the gateleg, make it so its top rail (FIG. 7-15B) has ¼-inch clearance below the wall rail, the upright goes to the bottom of the wall upright, and the leg is long enough to reach from the floor to the underside of the top, when that is horizontal (FIG. 7-15C). At this stage it will be advisable to mark on the wall where the table will come, so you can cut the leg length to suit.

You could join the gateleg parts with mortise and tenon joints, but it would be satisfactory to use ½-inch dowels, with three in each joint (FIG. 7-16C).

If you prefer a bracket, make it with similar upright and horizontal parts to the gate, but with the table support (FIG. 7-14H and 7-17B) projecting upwards enough to

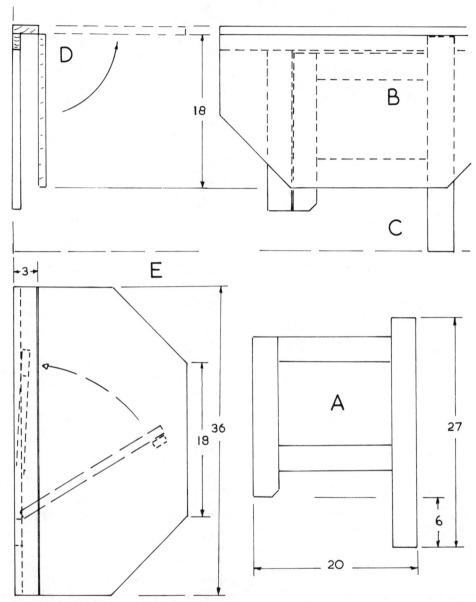

Fig. 7-15. Suggested sizes for the fold-down table.

level the table, and the lower part extending downwards enough to take the diagonal brace. Join these parts with dowels.

The simplest way to hinge the top is with three or four plain hinges underneath, so the top swings down, leaving the square edges exposed (FIG. 7-15D). This may not matter, but you might consider using a rule joint, if you have a suitable pair of planes or router cutters to work the two moldings.

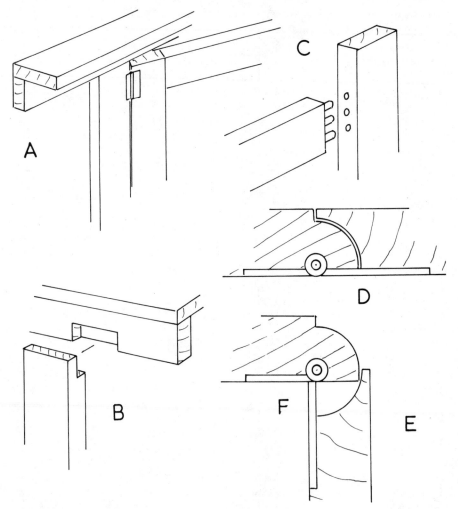

Fig. 7-16. Assembly details of parts of the fold-down table and a suggested use of a rule joint between top parts.

A rule joint gets its name from its similarity in section to the joint of an old twofold rule. When the top is in the up position, its edge covers a molded edge on the rear part (FIG. 7-16D). In the hanging position the molded edge is exposed, without a gap, and the appearance of the molding could match a molding on the table edge (FIG. 7-16E).

The important parts are back-flap hinges (FIG. 7-16F), which let into the edges with their knuckles upwards. They are designed to swing back further than normal hinges, and they are wide enough to have extra screws each side.

It is advisable to mark out the sections of wood for a rule joint fullsize, including the hinges. The centers of the curves of the matching wood edges must be the centers of the hinge pins, then movement of one curve over the other is smooth and the gap is minimal.

The tabletop is the most prominent part and its surface and edges require some thought. Its shape is important. You could have a simple rectangle, but in a restricted area the corners could be a nuisance. On the example, corners are shown cut away so the shape is almost part of an octagon (FIG. 7-15E). You may prefer to have smaller corner bevels, if you want more working area.

A curved front is attractive, and part ellipsis (FIG. 7-17) usually looks better

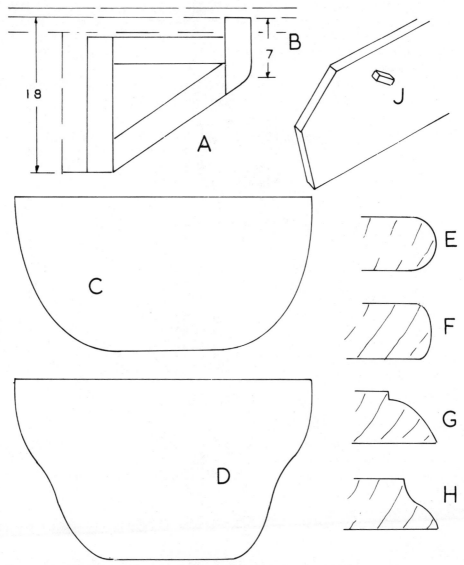

Fig. 7-17. A bracket and suggested top treatments for the fold-down table.

than a curve based on parts of a circle. You may choose a more intricate curve (FIG. 7-17D), particularly if you have a suitable router molding cutter to follow the shape.

The table edges could be left square. This may be better for a kitchen or utility room, where you may wish to clamp equipment over the edge. If you shape the edges, carry the same molding over the end of the piece attached to the wall. Fully rounding (FIG. 7-17E) may match other furniture, but a partial rounding (FIG. 7-17F) looks better. If you are using a rule joint between the top and its support, the edge molding should match the appearance of the meeting surfaces (FIG. 7-17G). Otherwise you may mold with any cutter you have (FIG. 7-17H).

Drill the wall parts to suit strong parts in the wall. Check that the attacted parts are parallel and square to the floor. Hinge the gateleg or bracket to its upright and try its movement. Hold the tabletop in place and note where the end of the support comes near the midpoint under the top. Screw on a block there (FIG. 7-17J) to act as a stop.

You may wish to separate the parts before finishing them with stain and polish. Hinge the parts together to complete the fold-down table.

Materials List for Fold-down Table

1 back strip	1 × 2 × 38
1 upright	1 × 3 × 24
1 top	1 × 18 × 38
gateleg	
1 upright	1 × 3 × 24
1 leg	1 × 3 × 29
2 rails	1 × 3 × 18
bracket	
1 upright	1 × 3 × 20
1 rail	1 × 3 × 18
1 upright	1 × 3 × 10
1 brace	1 × 3 × 24

8

Outdoor Equipment

If you have a yard, garden, patio, or deck, there are many items of furniture that you can make for use outdoors. If these are intended to remain outside, they need to be robust and able to resist the effects of weather. If you are able to store them under cover, they can be more like indoor furniture. There is an advantage in being able to reduce sizes for storage, by folding or taking apart. In general, outdoor furniture may be of simpler construction than similar items for permanent use indoors, so even if the wood sections may be larger, the work involved could be easier.

The greatest need outdoors is for seating and tables. Some which are suitable are described in Chapters 2 and 3. Many designs for indoor furniture can be adapted for outdoor uses. The furniture described in this chapter is unsuitable for inclusion in other chapters.

Some woods are durable and may be left outside during all weathers, but most woods need treatment to prevent the entry of water and the onset of rot. In some places they may need protection against boring insects. Many softwoods are susceptible to rot if they are unprotected, but the very resinous species may have more natural resistance. A few hardwoods, such as some oaks, will last a long time outdoors without special treatment.

Paint provides some protection, but it needs constant touching up. It is applied mainly for appearance. Better protection against rot and borers comes from soaking the wood in a preservative. It is possible to buy wood already treated with preservative, and this achieves a far better penetration than you can get by applying preservative with a brush. Most preservatives are poisons. Observe all the precautions and instructions provided with the type you choose. If you intend to use glue in the furniture and you buy the wood already treated, make sure the preservative is compatible with your glue. If you want to paint over the preservative, check that this is possible. You can get colored preservatives and use them without paint. Allow preservatives ample time to dry and for the smell to disperse before using treated furniture.

MOBILE FIREWOOD RACK

Logs cut for your wood-burning stove take up a fair amount of space and should be stacked for neatness and so they will dry. A few stakes in the ground may keep the pile in check, but as you use the logs, the remainder tend to be scattered. Leaving them on the ground limits drying. It is better to have a rack which keeps the firewood above the ground. This rack (FIG. 8-1) does that and it can be moved about. You may not want to wheel a full load very far, but you can reposition your stack of logs in the yard or bring them closer to the house after cutting them.

Sizes suggested (FIG. 8-2A) can be altered to suit your needs, but be careful to

Fig. 8-1. A mobile firewood rack allows you to store and move logs with the same piece of outdoor furniture.

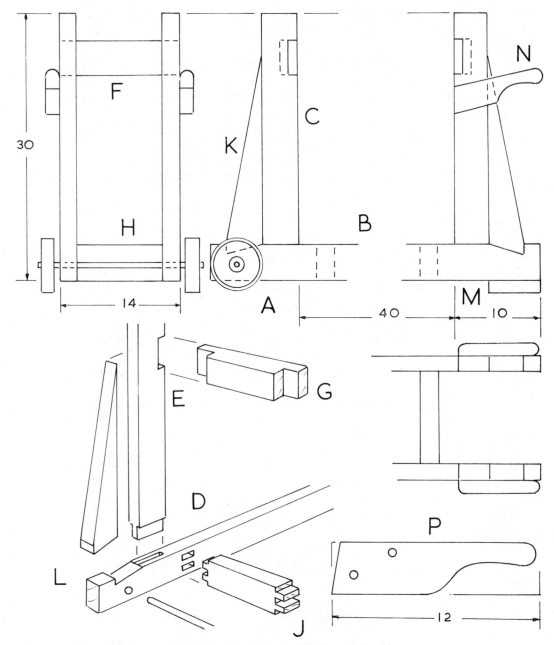

Fig. 8-2. Sizes and constructional details of the mobile firewood rack.

avoid too great a height in relation to the width, for the sake of stability. Most of the parts are from 2-inch × 4-inch wood. If you use softwood, treat it with preservative. It may be advisable to get the wheels first, in case you need to modify sizes to suit them. Those suggested are 6-inch diameter and 1½-inch wide on a

¾-inch axle. Iron wheels with flat rims may be preferable to lighter wheels with tires, as the load can be considerable and the flat rims spread the pressure over soft ground.

It would be possible to dowel most parts together. In a simple construction you could overlap parts and nail or screw them. For a better construction, mortise and tenon and halving joints are suggested, all joined with waterproof glue; you may also strengthen with nails, screws, or bolts.

Make the two sides of the base (FIG. 8-2B). Mark the positions of the uprights and crossbars, but leave details of the joints until the other parts are ready.

Cut the four uprights (FIG. 8-2C). Allow for tenons one-third the thickness and 1½-inch long at the bottom (FIG. 8-2D) and halving joints for the upper crossbars (FIG. 8-2E).

Make the upper crossbars (FIG. 8-2F), with ends halved to go across the uprights (FIG. 8-2G). Cut the uprights to suit.

The lower crossbars (FIG. 8-2H) are the same as the upper crossbars between shoulders. The tenons (FIG. 8-2J) could go through the base sides or be cut short. Make the mortises to suit.

The upright supports prevent the load forcing the uprights outwards. Make them 24 inches long (FIG. 8-2K). Notch the bottoms into the base sides (FIG. 8-2L).

Drill the sides for the axle.

Join the uprights to the base sides. At the same time, add the upright supports. Use plenty of waterproof glue and drive nails or screws from the supports into the upright. Check that the uprights finish square to the base and opposite assemblies match.

Join these parts with the crossbars, with plenty of glue and nails or screws into the halving joints. You could also drive nails or screws downwards through the tenons.

Try the wheels and axle in position. This will give you the height of packing blocks (FIG. 8-2M) to put under the opposite end to bring the rack level.

The handles (FIG. 8-2N) have to be arranged at a height convenient for yourself. The projecting parts must be shaped to provide a convenient grip, but do not reduce them any more than necessary (FIG. 8-2P). Fit them with glue and ½-inch bolts through.

Obviously, this rack does not require a high degree of finish, but taking sharpness off edges and corners limits the risk of splitting or splintering. Treat with preservative or paint.

Materials List for Mobile Firewood Rack

2 base sides	2 × 4 × 62
4 uprights	2 × 4 × 30
4 crossbars	2 × 4 × 16
4 supports	2 × 4 × 26
2 handles	1½ × 3 × 14

RECLINER

Some form of portable bed or lounger allows you to sunbathe or rest in the yard or on a patio, without being directly on the ground. This recliner (Fig. 8-3) is a full-length bed with its upper end able to tilt up to about 45°. When out of use, the tilting head will fold flat so the recliner will take up minimum space when stood on end or edge against a wall in a garage or elsewhere. There are handles at one end and wheels at the other, so the bed may be moved about easily. The base is made of boards across to support cushions.

Softwood may be used and the main parts are 2 inch × 3 inch section, with 1-inch × 7-inch boards on top. Wheels should be about 7-inch diameter and it is helpful if they are wide, so they are less likely to sink into soft ground. Their axle will probably be ¾-inch diameter. It is advisable to get the wheels and axle before starting work, as they control some of the sizes.

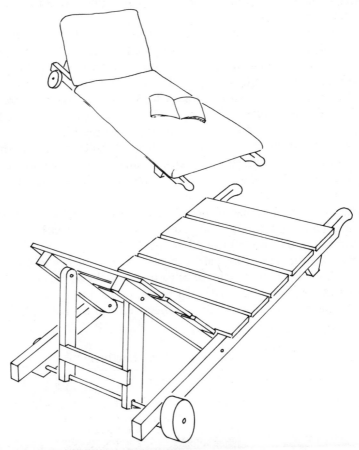

Fig. 8-3. A recliner that can be moved about or folded flat allows you to relax comfortably in the yard.

Construction may be with screws or nails and waterproof glue. Start with planed wood. If the recliner will be kept under cover when out of use, it need not be treated with preservative, but it will look more attractive if given a painted finish.

There are three assemblies. The main bed (FIG. 8-4A) forms the base. The head (FIG. 8-4B) has sides which fit inside the base sides. The strut assembly (FIG. 8-4C) fits inside the head sides and links to the axle when the head is raised. To fold the recliner the struts swing inside the head, which then swings inside the base (FIG. 8-4D). Start by making the base, then make the other parts in turn to fit within its end.

Make the two sides of the base (FIG. 8-4E). Fit blocks for the axle underneath (FIG. 8-4F). Drill to suit the axle. Use a wheel to check the height the base will be above the ground. Put support blocks (FIG. 8-4G) near the other end to raise it to the same height.

Shape the handles (FIG. 8-4H and 8-5). Thoroughly round the sections to make comfortable grips.

All crosswise boards are the same length, so cut them to match at the same time (FIG. 8-4J). If you do not use the suggested widths of 7 inches, make up about the same area with other widths, having spaces about 1-inch wide.

Drill the sides for the head pivots, which may be ½-inch carriage bolts.

Join the sides with boards across. Check that the base sides are kept parallel and the boards are square. The edge of the board near the pivot bolt should be about ½-inch forward of it to allow clearance for the tilted head sides.

Make the two head sides (FIG. 8-4K). Drill for bolts and round the lower end.

When you attach the boards across, arrange the distance over the outsides of the side pieces to fit easily between the sides of the base—up to ¼ inch will be acceptable.

The strut assembly has to fit between the sides of the head with a similar clearance. Make the sides (FIG. 8-4L). At the lower end drill each to fit the axle, then open this into a slot. Round the other end.

Join the strut sides with a strip across, let into notches to provide stiffness.

Put the axle through temporarily, then use loose bolts while testing the folding and opening action. You will probably need to counterbore for the bolt heads on the tops of the head sides, so they will clear the base sides when folding.

Materials List for Recliner

2 head sides	2 × 3 × 39
2 strut sides	2 × 3 × 27
9 boards	1 × 7 × 29
1 strut rail	1 × 3 × 20
2 wheel blocks	2 × 3 × 12
2 legs	1 × 7 × 12

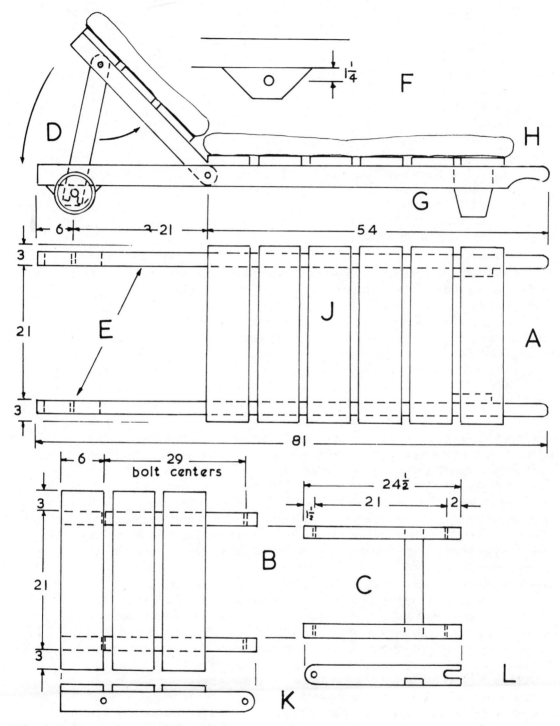

Fig. 8-4. Sizes and parts of the recliner.

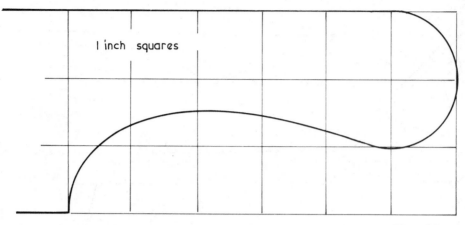

Fig. 8-5. Shape of a handle for the recliner.

If the action is satisfactory, separate the parts, remove sharp edges and corners, then paint all wood before final assembly. If it is a steel axle, protect that with paint.

Assemble with washers under the nuts. Locknuts will prevent loosening, but you are unlikely to fold and unfold enough to cause ordinary nuts to loosen noticeably.

BARBECUE TROLLEY/TABLE

For a barbecue the large quantities of food, equipment, plates, and cutlery all have to be brought to the yard. Additionally, the cook needs somewhere to put these things and a table or working surface for cutting, preparation, and serving. This trolley/table (FIG. 8-6) is intended to serve all these purposes. When out of use it can be folded flat.

The framework has four legs and some lengthwise pieces, two of which extend to form handles. The crosswise rails are divided and hinged, so they allow folding. The tabletop and a tray below may be lifted out, but when in place, they prevent accidental folding. At the opposite end to the handles are a pair of wheels, so the unit can be moved about. Suggested sizes (FIG. 8-7) should suit most needs, but they can be altered without affecting the method of construction.

It is advisable to use straight-grained hardwood for the framework. The tabletop could be plywood, possibly with a laminated plastic surface. The tray could be softwood with a plywood bottom. Almost any type of wheels could be used, but broad wheels about 5 inches diameter would roll well over varied surfaces. Get the wheels and axle before making the wood parts.

Mark out the two pairs of legs first (FIG. 8-8A). At the wheel end, cut the legs to clear the ground and mark the position of the axle to give the same total height as the other legs. Mark where the hinged rails will come. The handled rails will be screwed on the outside, but allow for the lower rails being doweled (FIG. 8-8B).

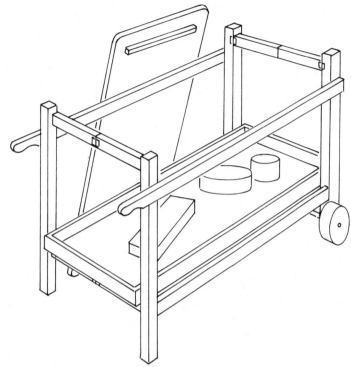

Fig. 8-6. *This barbecue trolley/table provides a working surface and storage as well as transport for food. When out of use the assembly folds flat.*

Make the lower rails (FIG. 8-7A) and prepare the ends and legs for dowels.

Prepare the handle rails to overlap the legs and extend 5 inches. Shape the extensions and well round them to form handles.

Assemble the pair of sides. Use glue and two screws arranged diagonally on each handle rail joint. Check squareness. Drill axle holes.

Cut the eight crosswise rails (FIGS. 8-7B and 8-8C). It is important for accurate assembly that they are exactly the same length with squared ends.

Use strong 2-inch hinges to join pairs of rails to each other and to the legs (FIG. 8-7C). Do not let the hinges into the wood. Make sure when the unit is in use the wood surfaces bear against each other, so the load is not taken only by the hinge knuckles.

Check that the assembly is square in all directions.

Make the top (FIG. 8-7D) to fit easily between the legs and extend about ½ inch at each end. Round the outer corners.

Put strips across the underside to fit inside the end crosswise rails, and keep the top in position while also holding the rails properly extended (FIG. 8-8D). Cut the strips short enough to clear the hinges. Position them to make a fairly tight bit, but you should be able to lift off the top without much trouble.

Make the tray (FIGS. 8-7E and 8-8E) to the same size as the top. It is a box, which

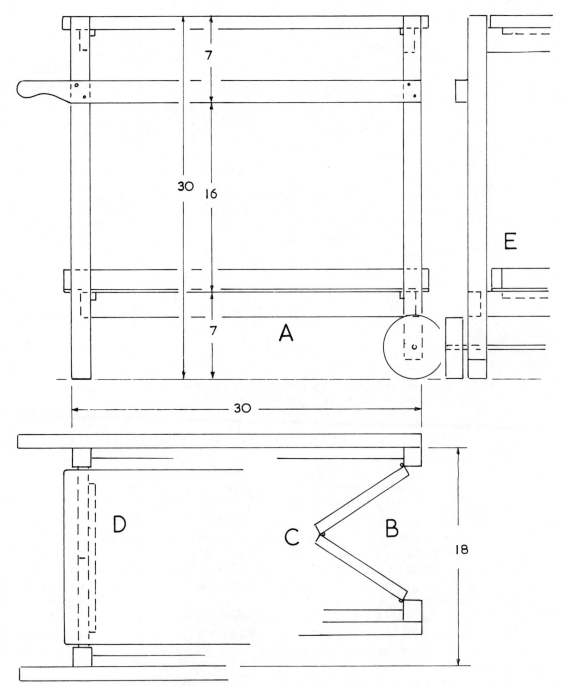

Fig. 8-7. Sizes and method of folding the barbecue trolley/table.

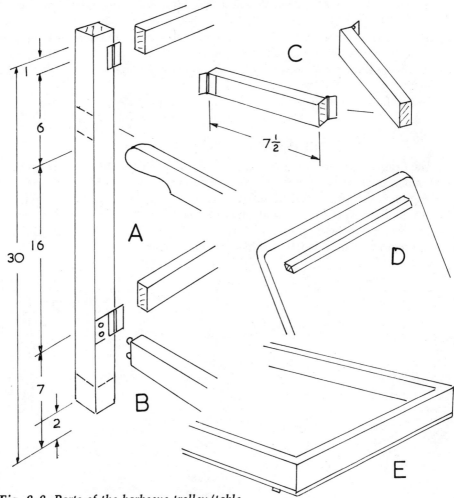

Fig. 8-8. Parts of the barbecue trolley/table.

Materials List for Barbecue Trolley/Table

4 legs	1½ × 1½ × 32
2 rails	1 × 2 × 28
2 handles	1 × 2 × 36
8 rails	1 × 2 × 9
1 top	1 × 15 × 32
2 tray sides	1 × 2 × 32
2 tray ends	1 × 2 × 16
1 tray bottom	15 × 32 × ¼ plywood

can be made with any of the usual corner joints from nails or screws to finger or dovetail joints. Take sharpness off the top edges. Glue and screw on a plywood bottom. Add strips across underneath, similar to those under the top. With top and tray in position, the unit should form a rigid assembly that can be wheeled with a load and will serve as a good working table and storage rack near your barbecue stand or pit.

Finish the wood with waterproof varnish or paint.

FOLDING SEAT PICNIC TABLE

The ordinary picnic table that has to be left in position will often suffer from birds and animals making the seats dirty, so you have the bother of cleaning or covering them before you can sit down to a meal. This picnic table (Fig. 8-9) looks like the standard type, but the seats may be folded so they are protected by the tabletop (Fig. 8-10) when not in use. There are no catches or loose parts, and the seats are rigidly secured whether folded or opened for use.

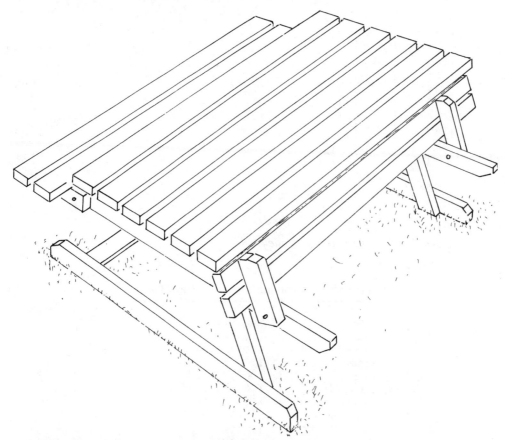

Fig. 8-9. This picnic table has seats which fold up and under the tabletop to protect them from the weather and animals.

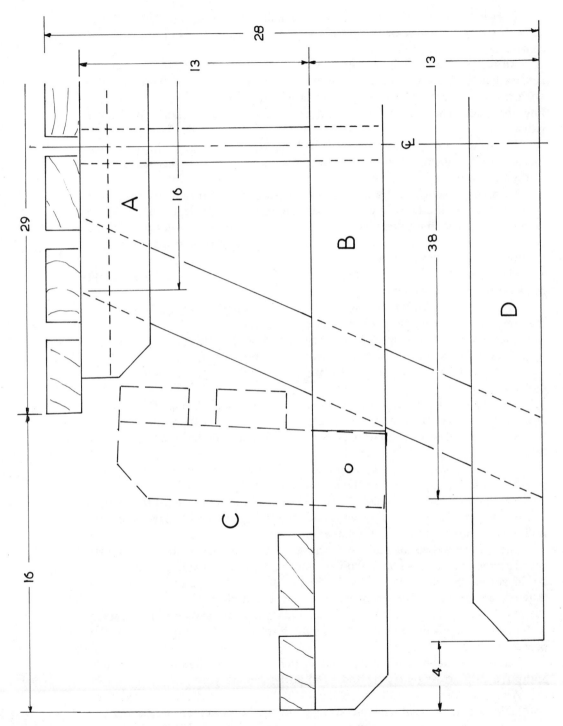

Fig. 8-10. Sizes of the main parts of the folding seat picnic table.

The suggested table covers a ground area of about 5 feet square. You can alter sizes to suit your needs or available space, while using the same method of construction.

All the parts are 2-inch × 4-inch section. Assembly might be with nails or screws, but bolts through major joints will ensure a strong table. You may also wish to use waterproof glue. Stagger bolts or screws, so they come in different lines of grain. The seat pivots should be ½-inch or larger bolts, preferably galvanized.

The sequence of construction starts with the two end frames, which are then joined with the tabletop strips and the diagonal braces, then the seats are added to fit the assembly.

Main sizes of the end frames are shown (FIG. 8-10). You may set out a half frame fullsize on the floor to get the sizes and angles of the legs, although it is possible to achieve the same results by putting down the horizontal parts in the correct relationship to each other, so you can lay a leg across to mark on it the lengths and angles, as detailed below.

Make the tops of the end frames (FIG. 8-10A and 8-12A). Bevel the ends and mark on the positions of the legs.

Cut the seat rails (FIG. 8-10B and 8-12B) to length and bevel the ends. Leave marking the hole positions until the seat strips are made.

Make the four seat strips (FIG. 8-10C and 8-12C), with bevels to match the seat rails. Drill the rails and the seat strips with matching holes for the pivot bolts.

Cut the two bases (FIG. 8-10D and 8-12D). Bevel the ends and mark the positions of the legs.

Lay one set of the horizontal parts on the floor parallel and at the correct spacing. Lay a piece of wood for a leg across and mark on it the positions of the horizontal parts. Use these markings as guides for marking and cutting the four legs.

Drill for bolts, screws, or nails and assemble the frames, with the horizontal pieces outside the legs. See that the assemblies match as a pair.

Cut the pieces for the tabletop and the seats all the same length (FIG. 8-11A). Remove any raggedness from the ends and take sharpness off all edges. Mark the positions of the frames across the tabletop pieces.

Mark the positions of nails and screws in the top pieces. In the simplest construction, you may nail on the top; or you could screw on with the screw heads left level with the top surfaces. For the best finish, counterbore for the screws so they can be sunk and their heads covered with glued plugs.

It will help in this first assembly if you temporarily nail on pieces of light scrap wood between the legs to hold them steadily in place while you get the first top pieces attached.

Join the end assemblies squarely to all the top boards, then invert the table and put a strip across (FIG. 8-11B and 8-12E) at the center.

While the assembly is still inverted, mark and cut the two diagonal braces (FIG. 8-11C). Notch over the seat rails and arrange notches at the center piece under the top so the brace ends meet. Nail or screw the braces in position. While working on

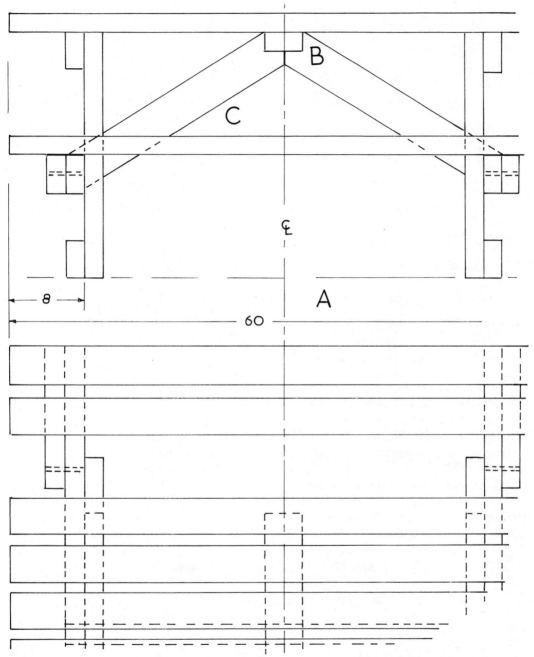

Fig. 8-11. Details of the lengthwise arrangements of the folding seat picnic table.

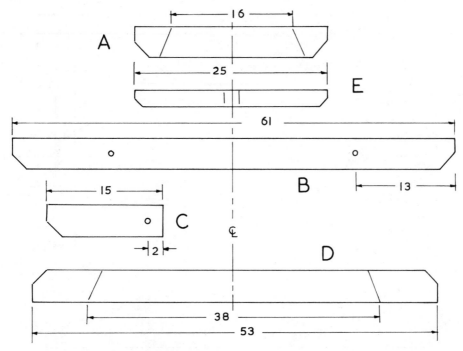

Fig. 8-12. Sizes of parts of the folding seat picnic table.

the braces, check squareness of the assembly. Once the diagonal braces are in place, the final shape cannot be altered.

Have the table the right way up to fit the seats. Arrange the supporting seat strips to come outside the seat rails with an easy fit. It may be advisable to fit the strips to the rails temporarily, then mark the strip positions on the seat tops. If the table is slightly out of square, the markings may be different on opposite sides, which will not matter, if you allow for it.

Join the seat tops to their strips in the same way as the tabletop strips were fitted. Check the seat folding action.

Remove any roughness or sharp corners. Finish with preservative or paint.

Materials List for Folding Seat Picnic Table

(all 2 inch by 4 inch section)

3 top strips	27 inches
2 seat rails	63 inches
2 bases	55 inches
4 seat strips	17 inches
6 table tops	62 inches
4 seat tops	62 inches
4 legs	35 inches
2 diagonal braces	32 inches

TOOL BOX/SEAT

It is helpful to be able to store your gardening tools near where you want to use them. It is also very pleasant to sit and contemplate your crops. This project (FIG. 8-13) is a box large enough to store the usual hand tools and some smaller power gardening tools. When closed it is a seat with back and armrests large enough to take three persons or for you to stretch out if overcome by your exertions. Sizes could be altered, but make sure you will be able to stow your long-handled tools.

The framing is solid wood, which could be hardwood or softwood treated with preservative. The box parts may be made of solid wood, possibly joined with waterproof glue or battens across to make up the widths, but it would be simpler to use exterior or marine grade plywood and finish with paint.

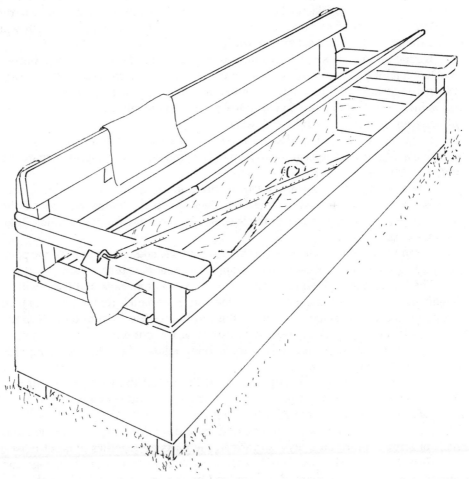

Fig. 8-13. This tool box/seat provides storage for garden tools as well as a seat for relaxation in the yard.

Many of the parts may be simply nailed or screwed together, but framework parts are better tenoned and halved, as suggested in the instructions, although you could dowel most of them, if you wish, using two 5/8 inch dowels in each 2 inch square end, preferably arranged diagonally.

The sizes suggested (FIG. 8-14) raise the bottom of the box about 3 inches above the ground. The seat should be a comfortable height, while providing plenty of space inside the box. The back and arms are not very high, but they should be adequate for the probable brief periods the unit will be used as a seat. If you alter sizes, see that the box top/seat will swing up without hindrance and can slope back enough against the back so it does not fall forward.

Start by making the two end frames (FIGS. 8-14A and 8-15A). Each consists of two legs joined by two rails and the arms. Make sure all inner surfaces are level, to provide clearance for the lifting seat.

Make the two rear legs (FIG. 8-14B). Taper from above the seat level to half width and cut away to take the back. Cut a notch to take the arm. This can be fairly shallow (FIG. 8-15B) as its purpose is to provide a location only, and strength will come from screws in the extending arm part outside.

Decide on the joints to be used and cut the four rails. If you are using mortise and tenon joints, allow for the tenons going at least 1 inch into each leg (FIG. 8-14C). When you assemble with waterproof glue, the joints may be further strengthened by 3/8-inch dowels across. If you use dowel joints, cut the rails to shoulder length to fit between the legs and drill for dowels.

Make the two front legs (FIG. 8-14D) and mortises at the same height as those on the rear legs. Cut tenons at the tops to fit the armrests (FIG. 8-14E) or prepare the ends for dowels.

The armrests (FIG. 8-14F and 8-15C) fit the notches in the rear legs and have mortises to take the tenons on the front legs. Keep the inner surfaces of the armrests level with the surfaces of the legs. Round the front and rear corners. Take sharpness off all edges.

Assemble the rails to the legs and fit the armrests, taking care to keep the parts square and without twist. See that the opposite ends match as a pair.

The box bottom will go through to rest on the bottom rails, but there will be lengthwise rails at the top edges of the back and front panels (FIG. 8-15D and E). To support these rails, arrange strips inside the end frames (FIG. 8-15F and G). Keep the lower ends high enough to clear the thickness of the bottom.

Prepare the tops of these pieces for halving joints. Make the two long rails with matching halved ends.

Make the bottom (FIG. 8-15H) notched to fit around the legs. Front and rear edges should be level with the strips on the end frames, and the ends should finish level with the outsides of the rails they rest on.

Join the end frames with the box bottom and the long rails, using glue and nails or screws. Work on a level surface so the parts go together without twist.

Close the ends with panels (FIG. 8-15J) level with the outsides of the legs, the top rail and with the bottom edges overlapping the box bottom by 1/4 inch.

Make the back (FIG. 8-15K) and front panels (FIG. 8-15L) to overlap the ends and

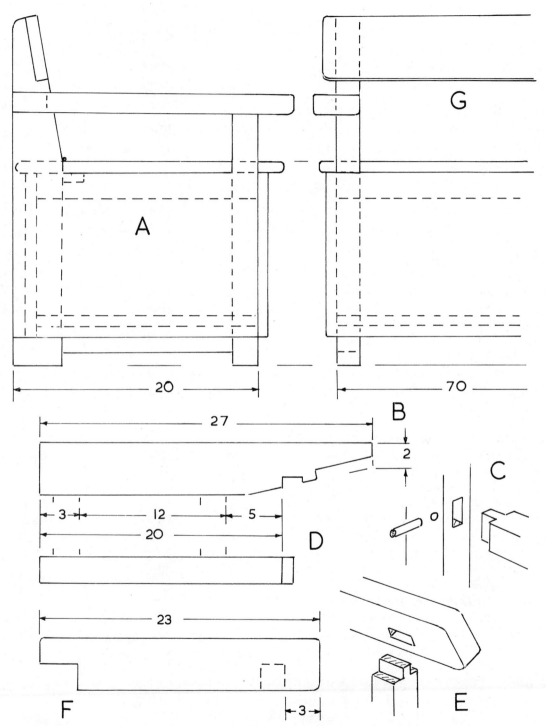

Fig. 8-14. Sizes and constructional details of the tool box/seat.

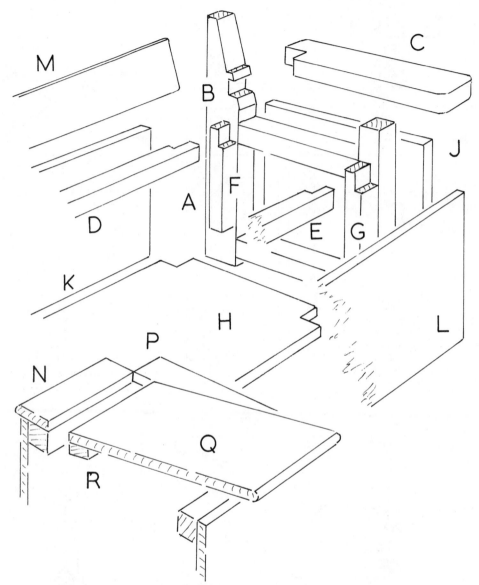

Fig. 8-15. Fitting the parts of the tool box/seat together.

with a bottom overlap to match the ends. Glue and screw all meeting surfaces. It should be satisfactory to screw into the edges of the bottom, but if you think your wood ought to be reinforced, stiffen the edges of the bottom with solid wood strips.

Make and fit the back (FIG. 8-14G and 8-15M). Let it overlap by 1 inch at the ends. Round its corners and take sharpness off the edges.

Cover the rear rail and back panel with a strip the same thickness as the seat

Materials List for Tool Box/Seat

2 front legs	2 × 2 × 23
4 end rails	2 × 2 × 16
2 long rails	2 × 2 × 68
2 inside pieces	2 × 2 × 14
2 armrests	2 × 4 × 25
1 back	1 × 5 × 74
1 seat stiffener	1 × 2 × 68
1 bottom	19 × 72 × ¾ plywood
1 back	15 × 74 × ¾ plywood
1 front	15 × 74 × ¾ plywood
2 ends	15 × 22 × ¾ plywood
1 seat	19 × 68 × ¾ plywood
1 seat strip	4 × 68 × ¾ plywood
2 seat strips	4 × 16 × ¾ plywood

(FIG. 8-15N), with its forward edge level with the rail and the front edges of the rear legs. It must not come behind this line, if the seat is to swing up properly.

Cover the end rails and panels with a similar strip between the legs (FIG. 8-15P). In both cases the strips may overlap the panels by ¼ inch to protect their edges from water which may enter the end grain.

Make the seat top (FIG. 8-15Q) to fit in the space, with a little clearance and an overlap of 1 inch at the front.

Stiffen its rear edge with a strip underneath (FIG. 8-15R) and hinge the parts together. You could use 2-inch or 3-inch hinges at about 18 inch intervals. For the simplest construction, screw them on the surface, but it will be neater to let them into the edges. In any case arrange the meeting edges fairly close to reduce the risk of rainwater entering.

You might make compartments or supports inside to suit particular tools, but it may be better to leave the inside clear to allow for changes in contents. The lid will stay down without any fastener, but you may fit a hasp and staple with a padlock if security is needed.

Paint all over, including the underside and bottoms of the legs. A light color inside will make the contents easier to see.

PERGOLA TABLE

A plant, preferably flowering, climbing over a pergola framework, makes an attractive feature in a garden or yard. It may be beside a path or be arranged over it, but in this case the pergola covers a table (FIG. 8-16), forming a bower in which meals can be taken. The tabletop is arranged to hinge, so when out of use it may be kept vertical (FIG. 8-17), which will be cleaner than leaving it level, and it then acts as a screen and part of the design when viewed from a distance. The table is at a normal height and is intended to be used with separate benches or chairs. There is standing headroom under the pergola top. As drawn (FIGS. 8-17 and 8-18), the unit covers a ground area about 5 feet by 6 feet and is just over 7 feet high. It is

Fig. 8-16. This pergola provides a structure for climbing plants above a table that can be folded to a vertical position when out of use.

designed to be freestanding, but if it is to stand on a lawn or other soft ground, you will probably wish to drive in pegs beside the base pieces and nail or bolt them in position; then the climbing plants may be in soil outside while there is grass between the uprights. On a hard surface you could bolt down and grow plants in large pots.

Nearly all the parts are 2-inch × 4-inch and 6-inch sections. You could cut joints between some parts, if you wish, but nailing should produce a sufficiently strong structure. However, you must remember that once the pergola has been covered with twining plants, you cannot take it down for repairs or move it, so make it strong enough to start with. Although parts are large, construction is simple and you should be able to make everything in a weekend; but if necessary

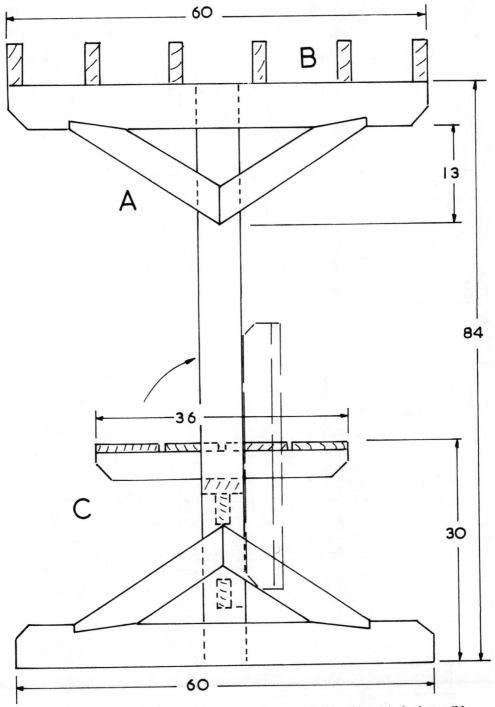

Fig. 8-17. Sizes of the end of the pergola table, showing the tabletop in both possible positions.

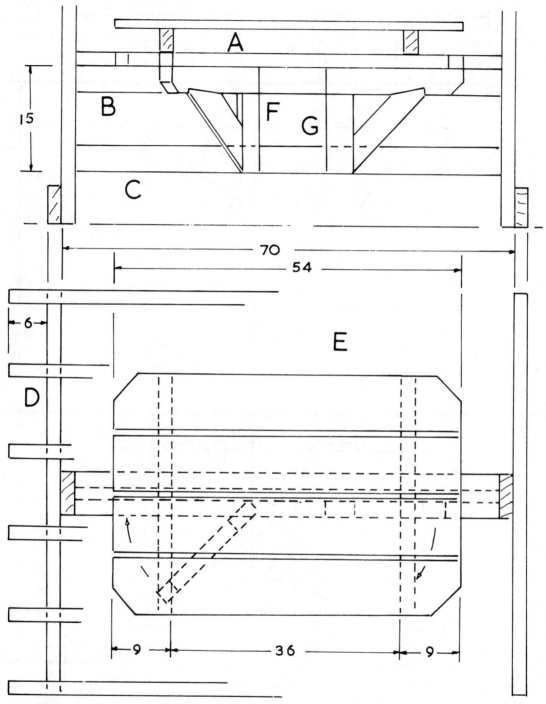

Fig. 8-18 *The pergola table structure with the tabletop in position supported on one bracket while the other is folded.*

you could build the pergola in one weekend, and add the tabletop and its brackets on another occasion.

For the strongest joints use stout nails that go almost through, with at least four in major crossings. You may find it advisable to nail from both sides. In many places, particularly near ends, drill undersize holes for the nails to reduce risks of splitting. Galvanized nails are preferable to plain nails, but unprotected nails should have a reasonably long life.

The best sequence of work is to first make the two end structures, then join them with the horizontal parts and finally make and fit the tabletop and its supporting brackets.

Prepare the parts for the two ends (FIG. 8-17). Note the assembled arrangements and sizes. Top and bottom horizontal pieces are nailed on the surfaces of the uprights and the diagonal struts are also on the surfaces of the uprights, but notched into the horizontal members. Tops and bottoms are the same.

Make the two uprights (FIG. 8-19A). Mark where other parts will cross. Locate the positions of the pieces that cross below the table. Mark where the diagonal struts come, but you will obtain the angles later.

Make the four pieces that will form the tops and bottoms (FIG. 8-19B). Bevel the ends and mark the position of each upright.

Put one of these pieces across the end of an upright and lay a piece of wood for a strut across (FIG. 8-17A and 8-19C), so you can mark where the strut comes on both parts. From this mark a notch 1 inch deep and cut the strut to fit in and allow it to reach the center of the upright. If this is satisfactory, mark and cut the notches and the struts.

Assemble the ends. Nail the horizontal pieces squarely to the uprights, then nail the struts into their notches and to the uprights. Be careful that the parts do not finish with a twist and that opposite ends match each other.

Prepare the parts that cross below the tabletop. You could tenon the ends into the uprights, but it is simpler to use cleats which are nailed both ways (FIG. 8-19D).

The piece that crosses flat is 6 inches wide, but the others are 4 inches wide.

The flat top piece (FIG. 8-18A and 8-19E) will have notches to take the top parts of the table brackets and will carry hinges to join the crossbars of the table. Mark both positions, but leave cutting until later assembly, when you may have to allow for slight variations. Put cleats across the ends.

Both lower pieces (FIG. 8-18B and C and 8-19F) are plain, but you can mark on where the bracket hinges will come. Put cleats on each side of the ends.

Nail the flat piece to the piece that goes under it, and nail all cleats to the main uprights. To hold the end assemblies while you do this, you will find it a help to temporarily nail strips of scrap wood across the tops of the structure.

Cut the strips that go across the top (FIG. 8-17B). They are shown 6 inches deep and at about 12-inch centers. For some plants it may be better to have them closer and you may find a 4 inch depth is stiff enough. A 6-inch overhang is shown (FIG. 8-18D), but you could make the pieces longer if you want a greater spread of foliage. Nail the pieces in place. If you want a positive location as you assemble, cut notches about ¼-inch deep at each crossing.

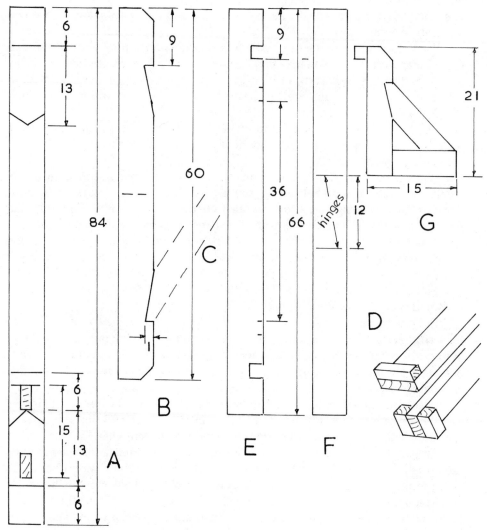

Fig. 8-19. Sizes of parts of the pergola table.

Check that the assembly will stand firm and level. Remove sharpness from edges, particularly where people may handle or knock against lower parts.

The tabletop is an assembly of boards over two crossbars (FIG. 8-17C, 8-18E and 8-20A). The suggested boards are about 1½ inches thick and 9 inches wide, but you could use other sections. Space evenly and round the outer edges and corners. Check the spacing of the crossbars against the positions for hinges marked on the supporting flat crosspiece. Use stout 2-inch hinges. Screw on temporarily to test the action, then remove the tabletop until the supporting brackets have been made and fitted.

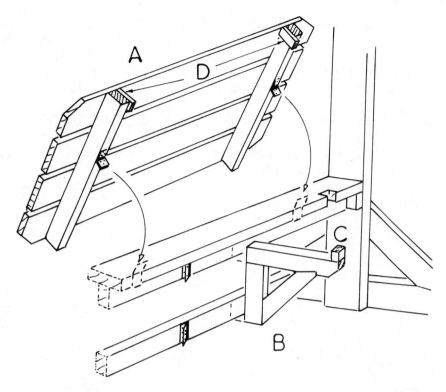

Fig. 8-20. Details of the pergola tabletop and the arrangement of folding brackets.

The supporting brackets (FIG. 8-18F and G) are shown hinged 12 inches apart. When the brackets are swung out they should come under the ends of the crossbars. If you have altered any sizes, you may have to alter the reach of the brackets. As shown, the ends of the brackets when folded will be hidden by the upright tabletop.

Materials List for Pergola Table

2 uprights	$2 \times 6 \times 86$
4 horizontal bars	$2 \times 6 \times 62$
8 diagonal braces	$2 \times 6 \times 30$
1 rail	$2 \times 6 \times 72$
2 rails	$2 \times 4 \times 72$
4 tabletops	$1\frac{1}{2} \times 9 \times 56$
2 table rails	$2 \times 4 \times 38$
2 bracket tops	$2 \times 4 \times 24$
2 bracket uprights	$2 \times 4 \times 15$
2 bracket struts	$2 \times 4 \times 20$
6 top strips	$2 \times 6 \times 88$

The height of each bracket (FIG. 8-19G and 8-20B) should match the spacing of the rails between the main uprights. Notch each upper end of a strut into the horizontal part, but the other joints could be nailed, or you may wish to use dowels and waterproof glue.

Nail a square block on each bracket that will support the tabletop level (FIG. 8-20C).

Hinge the brackets to their rails. Notch the flat rail so the blocks on the brackets will fit in level when the brackets are folded.

Try the action of the assembled table parts. Put stops on the table crossbars (FIG. 8-20D) to limit the movement of the brackets.

Finish the wood with paint or preservative, but avoid any treatment that might affect the plants.